D1244249

PRAISE FROM THE EXPERTS

"As stated in the introduction, this book is designed for people who need to perform financial economic research. It is neither a SAS primer nor a treatise on financial economic research; rather, it is a well-done work on how to perform the required analysis using the SAS language."

Robert Schechter
PhilaSUG Executive Committee Member

"I really enjoyed this book. . . . Everything is thoroughly explained and easy to follow. The examples are well chosen and teach the subject well."

Andrea Wainwright
Sr. SAS Programmer/Analyst

SAS Press

Using SAS®
in Financial
Research

Ekkehart Boehmer

John Paul Broussard

Juha-Pekka Kallunki

THE POWER TO KNOW.

The correct bibliographic citation for this manual is as follows: Boehmer, Ekkehart, John Paul Broussard, and Juha-Pekka Kallunki. 2002. *Using SAS® in Financial Research*. Cary, NC: SAS Institute Inc.

Using SAS® in Financial Research

ISBN-13: 978-1-59047-039-8
ISBN-10: 1-59047-039-7

SAS Institute Inc., SAS Campus Drive, Cary, North Carolina 27513.

1st printing, March 2002
2nd printing, December 2002
3rd printing, June 2005

SAS Publishing provides a complete selection of books and electronic products to help customers use SAS software to its fullest potential. For more information about our e-books, e-learning products, CDs, and hard-copy books, visit the SAS Publishing Web site at **support.sas.com/pubs** or call 1-800-727-3228.

CONTENTS

CHAPTER 5   EVENT STUDIES

CHAPTER 6   EFFECTIVE USE OF SAS MACROS: AN APPLICATION TO EVENT STUDIES

CHAPTER 7   ASSOCIATION TYPES OF STUDIES: INVESTIGATING THE PRICE-EARNINGS RELATIONSHIP

CHAPTER 8   PREDICTING BANKRUPTCY FROM FINANCIAL DISTRESS CHARACTERIZATION MODELS

CHAPTER 9   USING ACCOUNTING INFORMATION TO FORECAST MARKET PERFORMANCE

CHAPTER 10   ANALYSIS OF TRANSACTION DATA

ACKNOWLEDGMENTS

We are especially grateful to Judy Whatley and Donna Faircloth at SAS Institute for all their help and encouragement with the publication process. We also thank Carter Hill, Tapani Kovalainen, Markku Rahiala, and several anonymous other reviewers for their helpful comments. The chapter on financial distress would not have been possible without valuable insights and data from Panayiotis Theodossiou. This manuscript was largely completed while Dr. Boehmer was a Heisenberg Fellow of the German Science Foundation (DFG).

CHAPTER 1

INTRODUCTION

Introduction

This book is designed to provide a programming introduction for graduate students and other reasearchers of financial economics. We provide a strictly application-oriented introduction to using SAS to analyze a set of typical finance problems. For each of those problems, we provide a programming solution that uses a variety of features available in the SAS System. We discuss each program in detail and point out potential pitfalls. It is not our purpose to make a scientific contribution in finance, econometrics, or computer science. Rather, by providing a sound solution to each of our sample problems, we prepare readers to implement their own original ideas by extending our methodological groundwork. The book is designed such that by working through the chapters, readers assemble a toolkit of programming skills that enable them to find solutions to other and more complex empirical problems. We go beyond any other such book by focusing strictly on a selection of finance applications. This allows us to address specific issues that arise—for example, when merging return data with financial statement data, combining transaction-based trade prices with intraday bid-ask quotes, and then executing various hypothesis tests.

We also address several basic empirical methods that are frequently applicable in empirical financial research. We discuss various regression models, including OLS, logit, probit, and vector autoregressive models. We also show how to test for and correct for heteroscedasticity and autocorrelation. In addition, we program an event study and perform a variety of statistical tests. We also discuss discriminant analysis, variance ratio tests, and pooled cross-sectional and time-series models. In short, our programming examples cover a variety of approaches that should give the reader a firm starting point for several additional issues and for econometric extensions that go beyond the scope of this introductory book.

Although we briefly introduce almost every programming statement used in this text, we assume that the reader is familiar with the basic structure of the SAS language. Each SAS installation includes an in-depth online tutorial that is helpful in obtaining this basic working knowledge. We also assume that readers know how to access SAS from their platform of choice. SAS is largely platform independent; it is used in almost the same way whether on a PC, a mainframe, UNIX, or other system, and it provides a graphical user interface (GUI) or at least command menus on all platforms. We encourage every reader to use our sample programs and experiment with alternative programming statements, different options, and other data sets. Only continual practice will make statistical programming the highly efficient tool it was designed to be.

Generally, this book should be used in conjunction with SAS documentation. The online version (first available with Version 8) makes it easy to search for help and contains extensive documentation on the SAS language. SAS OnlineDoc contains a very detailed description of the econometrics and statistics associated with the SAS procedures. For this reason, we provide only brief references to methodological issues in this book. Similarly, the SAS Web site (www.sas.com) contains additional up-to-date technical reports and problem discussions by its staff and other users. Moreover, this Web site is probably the best place to search for specific methods or procedures that are not yet documented elsewhere. This book discusses only sample applications of certain language elements; for additional features, you should always consult SAS OnlineDoc.

Working with SAS

SAS software has a versatile display manager mode (driven by a GUI or by menus, depending on the operating system) that is helpful to access and explore data both interactively and in batch mode. The latter is generally more appropriate for more complex programming for data preparation and arrangement (and works most easily within the GUI). Because this is one of the major issues discussed in this book, we do not discuss interactive applications. Rather, we focus on the programming statements that are available in the DATA steps to manipulate, arrange, and analyze data. We also discuss PROC steps that are used to run preprogrammed routines (and may also have programming capabilities). To investigate a research question, most solutions involve combinations of several DATA and PROC steps. The DATA step and most procedures can be used to generate new data sets. These can then be used as input for the next set of SAS statements.

Each SAS program generates two types of reports: a *log* and an *output*. The SAS *log* contains the report of the execution of your program. The log is very important for verifying that programs have run error free, because this cannot always be seen from the output. The log contains several types of messages. For example, note messages report details of the execution, including the number of observations read from the source file and used in statistical procedures. Error messages indicate that the execution of the program was not completed because of errors in the program. Finally, warning messages indicate potentially ambiguous commands, which may or may not lead to incorrect or unexpected computations.

The *output* file contains the results of the program, such as estimation results or the printed contents of data sets.

Ground Rules

In SAS, each command must end with a semicolon, and each program must end with a RUN statement (a RUN is not necessary when more DATA or PROC steps follow—both imply a RUN statement). SAS is not sensitive to additional blanks, additional semicolons, or additional RUN statements. This relatively free format makes it easy to structure program files in ways that are straightforward to read. Comments may appear anywhere in a program and are enclosed between "*" and ";" or within "/*" and "*/".

After a SAS program is submitted for execution, the individual steps are executed sequentially: each step executes as soon as SAS either finds the beginning of the next DATA or PROC step or finds a RUN statement. In case of an error, the SAS log will most often display the exact location and reason for aborting the step (most syntax errors are already highlighted in red when you type the program using the SAS Program Editor). The most important skill to learn is to find programming errors based on the system's error messages. Because an error in one step will not necessarily prevent execution of subsequent steps, it may cause a flurry of errors in later steps even when their syntax is correct. This implies that to debug a program, it is most efficient to begin the search for errors at the beginning of the program, which is listed sequentially in the SAS log file. Correcting one error and running the program again may indeed resolve several error messages simultaneously.

One of the most important ground rules in empirical research is to always examine all intermediate results. For example, when a new data set is generated, it should be inspected before it is used for further computations. The inspection should be done visually and by computing descriptive statistics and, especially, by listing extreme values. Checking intermediate (and, of course, final) results is extremely important, because several programming errors or omissions follow the correct syntax and will not cause an error message to be generated. For example, several commonly used financial return databases code missing or dubious values as –99. This is reasonable because a financial return is, by definition, always larger than –1.0 and we can easily separate the error indicators from correct returns. Several colleagues tell tales of top-level publications in which someone forgot to check for these –99s and (puzzlingly) highly significant negative results were found. The only way to avoid this is to investigate any new data set very carefully.

SAS Data Sets

SAS has its own data storage system, the SAS data set, which all SAS procedures require as input. Data sets are organized in tabular form, where each record contains one observation and each column contains a field (variable). Large data sets can be associated with indexes for faster access. Data sets are ODBC (open database connectivity) compatible, so they can be accessed from and write to several popular database and spreadsheet programs. In a PC environment, for example, Microsoft Access tables can be saved directly as SAS data sets through ODBC. From inside SAS, each data set can be exported to formats such as Dbase or

Microsoft Excel (similar procedures are available for other platforms). Furthermore, the procedure CPORT is available if data sets have to be transferred between systems running SAS on different platforms. To keep the programming examples in this book platform independent, we will assume throughout that data files are in ASCII (text) format, although most users will store their data in database or spreadsheet programs. In general, one would use either menu commands or PROC IMPORT and PROC EXPORT to read and write non-SAS file formats.

Conventions Used in This Book

Each chapter is a self-contained discussion of a specific empirical issue and the program used to address it. Most contain a brief discussion of the underlying finance issues to put the sample analysis into perspective. At the beginning of each chapter, we list the major finance concepts that will be discussed and the type of data employed. Within the text, SAS commands and keywords appear in ALL CAPS. Variable names appear in SMALL CAPS.

The programs we discuss in each chapter are found at the end of that chapter. For easier reading, we divide each program into sections that we discuss individually within the chapter. Both the complete program listing and the individual sections can be used to practice and experiment with variations of the programs, but the sections must be submitted sequentially in their original order. In addition, we omit RUN statements within the chapters for brevity. To submit individual sections, a RUN statement must be included at the end of the section. Otherwise it will execute only after the next set of statements is submitted.

CHAPTER 2

RANDOM WALKING OR WALKING RANDOMLY: USING SAS TO CONDUCT VARIANCE RATIO TESTING OF ASSET PRICES

Key Concepts
• Test of random walk theory
• Variance ratio test
Data: Daily stock returns

Background for the Random Walk Theory of Asset Prices

Stock market efficiency has been debated by both academics and financial market practitioners. One particular form of stock market efficiency is informational efficiency, which relies on the premise that asset prices fully reflect all relevant available information instantaneously. Since the arrival of information is unpredictable, asset prices are also unpredictable. This fundamental assumption—that information arrival is random, and hence movements in asset prices are also random—is encompassed by the random walk theory of asset prices.

Simply, the random walk theory indicates that since information arrival is unpredictable, the best predictor of an asset's price is its current value. This straightforward idea is easily incorporated into the well-known random walk model of asset prices, which can be expressed as follows:

$$P_t = P_{t-1} + \varepsilon_r \tag{2.1}$$

where P_t is today's price, P_{t-1} is the previous period's price, and ε_r is a random error term. Each random error term represents the arrival of new information, which if unpredictable must be independent of each other. If a null hypothesis is made that the random error term is independent and identically normally distributed, then an important statistical fact results. This fact indicates that the variance of the random error term is linear in the time frame over which prices are observed. Simply, the variance of biweekly price changes should be twice that of weekly price changes. Moreover, the variance of monthly price changes should be four times that of weekly price changes, and so on. The linear relationship between the time interval of price observations and its variance is the essence of the straightforward specification test developed by Lo and MacKinlay (1988).

Lo and MacKinlay (1988) developed limiting distributions for variance ratio estimators, with and without the existence of heteroscedasticity, and showed that asset prices do not necessarily follow a random walk. Their estimators are defined as follows:

$$\hat{\mu} = \frac{1}{n} \sum_{k=1}^{n} (P_k - P_{k-1}) \tag{2.2}$$

$$\overline{\sigma}_a^2 = \frac{1}{n-1} \sum_{k=1}^{n} (P_k - P_{k-1} - \hat{\mu})^2 \tag{2.3}$$

$$\overline{\sigma}_q^2 = \frac{1}{m} \sum_{k=q}^{n} (P_k - P_{k-q} - \hat{\mu})^2$$
$$m = q(n-q+1)\left(1 - \frac{q}{n}\right) \tag{2.4}$$

Here, equation (2.2) represents the mean of n weekly price changes. Equation (2.3) represents a variance estimator for the weekly price changes, while equation (2.4) represents a variance estimator for q-weekly price changes. m is an adjustment made in the denominator of the q-weekly variance estimator to accommodate overlapping observations, and it helps increase the power of the variance ratio test. The variance ratio itself is defined as

$$\overline{M}_r = \frac{\overline{\sigma}_q}{\overline{\sigma}_a} - 1 \tag{2.5}$$

To accommodate heteroscedasticity, a standardized test statistic z^*, asymptotically distributed as a standard normal variate, was formulated:

$$z^* = \sqrt{n}\,\bar{M}_r \Big/ \sqrt{\hat{\theta}} \xrightarrow[asym]{} N(0,1)$$

where

$$\hat{\theta} = \sum_{j=1}^{q-1} \left[\frac{2(q-j)}{q} \right]^2 \hat{\delta}(j) \tag{2.6}$$

and

$$\hat{\delta}(j) = \frac{n \sum_{j+1}^{n} (P_k - P_{k-1} - \hat{\mu})^2 (P_{k-j} - P_{k-j-1} - \hat{\mu})^2}{(P_k - P_{k-1} - \hat{\mu})^2}$$

Equations (2) through (6) will be estimated in this chapter. Specifically, SAS DATA and PROC steps will be used to illustrate the flexibility SAS gives you in generating research results. It is hoped that you will gain an appreciation of the power of SAS and the valuable assistance it brings to your research efforts.

The Data

Data for this chapter follow that used in Lo and MacKinlay (1988). Specifically, the Center for Research in Security Prices (CRSP) daily equal weighted index is used to generate weekly price series, which is then used to replicate Lo and MacKinlay's (1988) variance ratio tests. Only the first row in Lo and MacKinlay's (1988) first table will be replicated, but the SAS code can easily be extended to accommodate additional data. The time period used in this chapter—September 6, 1962, through December 26, 1985—is that used in Lo and MacKinlay (1988).

Sample SAS Code for Variance Ratio Specification Testing

Reading the Data

As mentioned in the previous section, weekly price data from CRSP are used to calculate Lo and MacKinlay (1988) variance ratios to test the random walk model of price behavior. The code can be easily modified to incorporate different price series and time intervals. Our goal is to illustrate how SAS can be used in this type of research, so we leave it to the user to make the appropriate changes to fit the data at hand.

The sample code begins with basic routines to read in data from external files. Although comments are used to define tasks and variables used within the code, explicit clarifications will be made after each section of code.

Code 2.1: Reading price data and creating log-relative price changes

```
data weekly;
     * read weekly price and return data from CRSP;
     infile 'C:\weekly.output';
     input begwed endwed eindbeg eindend vindbeg vindend ewhpr vwhpr;
     *convert indexes to log prices;
     eindbeg = log(eindbeg);
     eindend = log(eindend);

     *create log-relative weekly changes in the indexes;
     ehpr = eindend - eindbeg;

     *create log-relative 2-week changes in the indexes;
     ehpr2 = eindend - lag1(eindbeg);

     *create log-relative 4-week changes in the indexes;
     ehpr4 = eindend - lag3(eindbeg);

     *create log-relative 8-week changes in the indexes;
     ehpr8 = eindend - lag7(eindbeg);

     *create log-relative 16-week changes in the indexes;
     ehpr16 = eindend - lag15(eindbeg);

     keep ehpr ehpr2 ehpr4 ehpr8 ehpr16;
```

In the first statements of this DATA step, dates and index values are read to the data set WEEKLY from an external file named WEEKLY.OUTPUT. The following variables are in the external data set:

BEGWED	date of first Wednesday in the data series
ENDWED	date of subsequent Wednesdays in the data series
EINDBEG	CRSP equal weighted index for the beginning of each week
EINDEND	CRSP equal weighted index for the end of each week

As you can see, the external data set contains date values for each Wednesday throughout the time series. These values are not needed for the analysis, but were required to retrieve data from CRSP. A sample SAS program that generates Wednesday dates as an input for the program that reads data from CRSP is presented at the end of this chapter.

After reading the appropriate index date from the external file, SAS generates weekly log-relative price change variables. To accomplish this task, we first use the SAS log(x) function, which takes the natural logarithm of the argument within the parentheses. Next, we take the differences between weekly observations by subtracting the index value at the beginning of the week from its value at the end of the week. Longer interval price relatives are generated using the

SAS LAG*n(x)* function.[1] Note that *n* defines the lag length for the function (it can be omitted for *n*=1). The following variable names are used:

```
EHPR        weekly price changes for CRSP equal weighted index
EHPR2       biweekly price changes for CRSP equal weighted index
EHPR4       4-weekly price changes for CRSP equal weighted index
EHPR8       8-weekly price changes for CRSP equal weighted index
EHPR16      16-weekly price changes for CRSP equal weighted index
```

Since the only variables of interest are the log-relative price changes, the last SAS command, KEEP, instructs SAS to write these only to the output data set WEEKLY. Note that the DATA step concludes with a RUN statement. At least one RUN statement is necessary at the end of the entire program, but each DATA and PROC step may optionally be ended with a RUN statement as well. To make the partial programs we discuss in the main text self-contained, we will include the RUN statement in each segment.

Generating Estimates for the Estimators

Now that we have generated the appropriate variables, we need to generate estimates, or values for each of the Lo and MacKinlay estimators. The first step in that process uses the SAS procedure PROC MEANS.

Code 2.2: Computing the average index return

```
proc means data=weekly n mean std var noprint;
    var ehpr;
    output out=muhat mean = muhat n = nq;
```

Because we are not necessarily interested specifically in the mean of the weekly price changes, we use the option NOPRINT. This option tells SAS not to print the results of the procedure. We are interested, however, in two pieces of information—the mean of the data series of weekly price changes; and the number of observations, or the weekly time periods used as the base number of observations in the variance ratio testing sections. As you can see from equation (2), the estimator for the series mean, $\hat{\mu}$, is simply an average of the data series, which is what SAS calculates through PROC MEANS.

To capture the two pieces of interest, the mean and the number of observations, we use an OUTPUT statement, which creates a new data set named MUHAT. MUHAT contains two variables of interest—an estimate of the sample mean, also named MUHAT; and the number of observations, which is named NQ (we do not name the variable N, as in the model discussed above, to distinguish it from the SAS keyword N). These values will be used later in generating and testing the variance ratios.

---

[1] Obviously, we could have generated the same result using a single price series instead of one that had beginning and ending weekly price values.

The next step required in calculating variance ratios is to generate information associated with biweekly price changes. This task is shown in the next section of SAS code.

Code 2.3: Computing squared deviations from mean returns

```
data weekly2;
    if _n_ = 1 then set muhat;
    set weekly;
    sigatop = ((ehpr - muhat)**2);
    sigatopl = lag1(sigatop);
    deltop = sigatop * sigatopl;
    delbot = sigatop;
    sigctop = ((ehpr2 - 2*muhat)**2);
```

This DATA step of the SAS program introduces a useful technique: merging summary information with many observations. The first line of code causes the summary data generated by PROC MEANS to be "set" next to each observation of the original data series. This allows us to calculate the variance estimate for the biweekly variance estimator found in equation (4). The variables are defined as follows:

```
SIGATOP      Squared deviations from the mean return
SIGATOPL     Lagged squared deviation from the mean return
DELTOP       Product of current and lagged squared deviation (equation 6)
DELBOT       The denominator used in estimating delta
SIGCTOP      Squared deviation from twice the mean return (for biweekly variance
             estimates)
```

The next task is to generate the necessary statistics for calculating the variance ratio of the biweekly price changes.

Code 2.4: Computing sums of squared deviations from mean returns

```
proc means data=weekly2 noprint;
    var sigatop sigctop deltop delbot;
    output out=varrat2 sum = sigatop sigctop deltop delbot;
```

As you can see, the code used here is similar to that used to generate the summary statistics for the weekly price change data. The PROC MEANS here generates sums for each of the numerator and denominator terms for the variance estimates. The sums are stored in the data set VARRAT2, which will be used to calculate the variance ratio for the biweekly price changes. The actual calculations for the variance ratio estimates are located in Code 2.5. Whenever PROC MEANS creates an output data set, it adds the automatic variable _FREQ_, which represents the number of observations used to compute the requested statistics. (Note: If some variables have missing values, the number of nonmissing observations can be produced using the keyword N=.) In this example, _FREQ_ corresponds to the term NQ, as in equation (2).

Code 2.5: Computing variance ratio and the associated test statistic

```
data varrat2;
    set varrat2;
    nq = _freq_;
    q = 2;  qm1 = q - 1;
    j = 1;
    theta=0;
    m = q*(nq-q+1)*(1-q/nq);
    siga = sigatop/(nq-1);
    sigc = sigctop/m;
    varrat2 = sigc/siga;
    delta = nq*deltop/(delbot**2);
    do until (j > qm1);
        theta = theta + ((2*(q-j)/q)**2)*delta;
        j+1;
    end;
    z = sqrt(nq)*(varrat2-1)/sqrt(theta);
    keep nq varrat2 z;
    label
    nq = "Number of Weekly Returns"
    varrat2 = "Variance Ratio for 2 Week Returns"
    z = "Heteroskedastic Robust Test Statistic";

proc print data=varrat2 label noobs;
```

The section of the program shown in Code 2.5 defines a few new variables, which are defined as follows:

NQ	The number of base weekly price changes
Q	The number of weekly multiples for the price changes
J	Counter for the autocorrelation process
THETA	Variable representing variance of variance ratio estimator
M	Adjustment factor to denominator of biweekly variance estimate
SIGA	Variance of weekly price changes
SIGQ	Variance of biweekly price changes
VARRAT2	Variance ratio of biweekly to weekly price changes
DELTA	Used in calculating variance of variance ratio estimator
Z	Test statistic for variance ratio estimate—robust to heteroscedasticity

Since the only variables of interest are the number of weekly returns (NQ), the variance ratio (VARRAT2), and the test statistic (Z*), the KEEP statement is used. Also, labeling the variables is accomplished via the LABEL statement.

After calculations have been made, we need to "see" the estimates. This is done with PROC PRINT. Selecting the LABEL option to the procedure allows the previously defined labels to be associated and printed with the pertinent variables. The NOOBS option deletes the observation number associated with this data set, which is a nuisance variable for our purpose. The results of PROC PRINT are as follows.

Output 2.1: Variance ratio test for a 1-week lag

```
                          The SAS System

          Number of        Variance        Heteroscedastic
           Weekly         Ratio for 2         Robust Test
           Returns        Week Returns         Statistic

             1216           1.29512            7.51232
```

This output matches exactly the first line of the first table found in Lo and MacKinlay (1988). The implication is that since the variance ratio is statistically different from 1.0 (that is, 1.3), there appears to be a rejection of the random walk theory in that approximately 30% of a current period's price change can be explained by the last period's price change. This result implies that price changes are not random and hence contain some level of predictability. Comparing the *t*-test statistic to the standard normal distribution, we see that the estimate is more than seven standard deviations away from zero, and therefore is highly significant.

Now that we have generated the variance ratio for the biweekly variance over the weekly variance, we will calculate the variance ratio for a 4-week price change over the weekly variance. The statements used here are quite similar to those used in the biweekly variance ratio calculation. The main difference is the use of more *lagged* variables for calculating the delta estimate found in equation (2.6).

First, the code for generating observations used in estimating variances and delta and theta estimates is found in the following DATA and PROC MEANS steps (Code 2.6).

Code 2.6: Computing squared deviations from the mean and their sums for 4-week lags

```
data weekly4;
    if _n_ = 1 then set muhat;
    set weekly;
    sigatop = ((ehpr - muhat)**2);
    deltop1 = sigatop * lag1(sigatop);
    deltop2 = sigatop * lag2(sigatop);
    deltop3 = sigatop * lag3(sigatop);
    delbot = sigatop;
    sigctop = ((ehpr4 - 4*muhat)**2);

proc means data=weekly4 noprint;
    var sigatop sigctop deltop1 deltop2 deltop3 delbot;
    output out = varrat4
            sum = sigatop sigctop deltop1 deltop2 deltop3 delbot;
```

Next, the variance ratios and test statistics are generated.

Code 2.7: Computing 4-week variance ratios and test statistics

```
data varrat4;
    set varrat4;
    q = 4;  qm1 = q - 1;
    j = 1;
    theta=0;
    array deltaj(3) deltop1 -- deltop3;
    array delta(3);
    nq = _freq_;
    m = q*(nq-q+1)*(1-q/nq);
    siga = sigatop/(nq-1);
    sigc = sigctop/m;
    varrat4 = sigc/siga;
    do until (j > qm1);
            delta(j) = nq*deltaj(j)/(delbot**2);
            theta = theta + ((2*(q-j)/q)**2)*delta(j);
            j+1;
    end;
    z = sqrt(nq)*(varrat4-1)/sqrt(theta);
    keep nq varrat4 z;
    label
    nq = "Number of Weekly Returns"
    varrat4 = "Variance Ratio for 4 Week Returns"
    z = "Heteroscedastic Robust Test Statistic";

proc print data=varrat4 label noobs;
```

Notice that this section of the program introduces a new SAS statement. The ARRAY statement allows you to specify arrays that make computational tasks easier. For instance, the particular ARRAY statement used here associates the numerator values for the DELTA estimates with an array called DELTAJ, which contains the three numerators (each individual $\delta(j)$ from equation 2.6). These individual $\delta(j)$ estimates are then used to estimate the $\theta(j)$'s also found in equation (2.6), which are in turn used to generate the heteroscedastic consistent estimates of the variance ratio test statistic. Finally, PROC PRINT is used to write the estimates to the SAS output file.

Output 2.2: Variance ratio test for 4-week lags

Number of Weekly Returns	Variance Ratio for 4 Week Returns	Heteroscedastic Robust Test Statistic
1216	1.64105	8.88444

Here again, the results match Lo and MacKinlay's (1988) first-table estimates and imply a statistically significant rejection of the random walk model of asset price behavior.

Summary

The purpose of this chapter was to introduce you to how SAS can be used to test one of the most frequently discussed paradigms in financial economics, the random walk theory of asset prices. In particular, this chapter replicates Lo and MacKinlay's (1988) variance ratio test to illustrate the power and flexibility SAS provides in financial economics research. Granted, there are many different approaches to estimating Lo and MacKinlay's (1988) variance ratios. This chapter serves only as an introduction to the versatility of SAS. You can easily use the code discussed here as a stepping-stone to generate the 8-week and 16-week variance ratio estimates found in Lo and MacKinlay (1988). All that is required is adding additional lagged variables to each data set.[2] The complete code for generating the first set of Lo and MacKinlay's (1988) variance ratio estimates is presented in the following section.

Program Listing

Code 2.8: Program to generate Wednesday dates usable by CRSP

```
* get dates of all Wednesdays from 9-5-62 to 12-27-85;
* write date and that of the preceding week to a text file;
data _null_;
 format crspdate dtlag yymmddn8.;
 file 'weddateb';
 do crspdate=mdy(9,5,62) to mdy(12,27,85);
  if weekday(crspdate) = 4 then do;
   dtlag=crspdate-7;
   put dtlag +2 crspdate;
  end;
 end;
run;[eb1]
```

---

[2] You can also use the SAS macro facility to streamline program code. Using SAS macros will be the subject of Chapter 6, "Effective Use of SAS Macros: An Application to Event Studies."

Code 2.9: Program to generate Lo and MacKinlay's (1988) variance ratios

```
* program to calculate variance ratios;

data weekly;
    * read weekly price and return data from CRSP;
    infile 'C:\weekly.output';
    input begwed endwed eindbeg eindend vindbeg vindend ewhpr vwhpr;
    *convert indexes to log prices;
    eindbeg = log(eindbeg);
    eindend = log(eindend);

    *create log-relative weekly changes in the indexes;
    ehpr = eindend - eindbeg;

    *create log-relative 2-week changes in the indexes;
    ehpr2 = eindend - lag1(eindbeg);

    *create log-relative 4-week changes in the indexes;
    ehpr4 = eindend - lag3(eindbeg);

    *create log-relative 8-week changes in the indexes;
    ehpr8 = eindend - lag7(eindbeg);

    *create log-relative 16-week changes in the indexes;
    ehpr16 = eindend - lag15(eindbeg);

    keep ehpr ehpr2 ehpr4 ehpr8 ehpr16;

proc means data=weekly n mean std var noprint;
    var ehpr;
    output out=muhat
            mean = muhat
            n = nq;

data weekly2;
    if _n_ = 1 then set muhat;
    set weekly;
    sigatop = ((ehpr - muhat)**2);
    sigatopl = lag1(sigatop);
    deltop = sigatop * sigatopl;
    delbot = sigatop;
    sigctop = ((ehpr2 - 2*muhat)**2);
```

```
proc means data=weekly2 noprint;
    var sigatop sigctop deltop delbot;
    output out = varrat2
            sum = sigatop sigctop deltop delbot;

data varrat2;
    set varrat2;
    nq = _freq_;
    q = 2;   qm1 = q - 1;
    j = 1;
    theta=0;
    m = q*(nq-q+1)*(1-q/nq);
    siga = sigatop/(nq-1);
    sigc = sigctop/m;
    varrat2 = sigc/siga;
    delta = nq*deltop/(delbot**2);
    do until (j > qm1);
            theta = theta + ((2*(q-j)/q)**2)*delta;
            j+1;
    end;
    z = sqrt(nq)*(varrat2-1)/sqrt(theta);
    keep nq varrat2 z;
    label
    nq = "Number of Weekly Returns"
    varrat2 = "Variance Ratio for 2 Week Returns"
    z = "Heteroscedastic Robust Test Statistic";

proc print data=varrat2 label noobs;

data weekly4;
    if _n_ = 1 then set muhat;
    set weekly;
    sigatop = ((ehpr - muhat)**2);
    deltop1 = sigatop * lag1(sigatop);
    deltop2 = sigatop * lag2(sigatop);
    deltop3 = sigatop * lag3(sigatop);
    delbot = sigatop;
    sigctop = ((ehpr4 - 4*muhat)**2);

proc means data=weekly4 noprint;
    var sigatop sigctop deltop1 deltop2 deltop3 delbot;
    output out=varrat4
            sum = sigatop sigctop deltop1 deltop2 deltop3 delbot;
```

```
data varrat4;
    set varrat4;
    q = 4;   qm1 = q - 1;
    j = 1;
    theta=0;
    array deltaj(3) deltop1 -- deltop3;
    array delta(3);
    nq = _freq_;
    m = q*(nq-q+1)*(1-q/nq);
    siga = sigatop/(nq-1);
    sigc = sigctop/m;
    varrat4 = sigc/siga;
    do until (j > qm1);
            delta(j) = nq*deltaj(j)/(delbot**2);
            theta = theta + ((2*(q-j)/q)**2)*delta(j);
            j+1;
    end;
    z = sqrt(nq)*(varrat4-1)/sqrt(theta);
    keep nq varrat4 z;
    label
    nq = "Number of Weekly Returns"
    varrat4 = "Variance Ratio for 4 Week Returns"
    z = "Heteroscedastic Robust Test Statistic";

proc print data=varrat4 label noobs;
run;
```

CHAPTER 3

ANALYZING WINNERS AND LOSERS: USING SAS TO TEST THE OVERREACTION HYPOTHESIS

> **Key Concepts**
> - Winner and loser portfolios
> - Ranking securities by past returns
> - Long-term holding period returns
>
> **Data:** Monthly stock returns

Background on Behavioral Issues Specifically Related to Overreaction

Until the mid- to late 1980s, modern financial economics research could be summed up as investigating the interaction between rationally behaving utility maximizers. *Homo economicus* activity dominated research articles, and little investigation into individual market participant behavior was produced. With the influences of clinical psychology and experimental economics impacting the finance discipline from different angles, however, research into the behavioral aspects of finance began to emerge. One of the first empirical articles in the behavioral finance area was DeBondt and Thaler's (1985) seminal study on stock market overreaction.

DeBondt and Thaler's results showed that over long holding period horizons, stocks appear to register significant price reversals. This is in stark contrast to the price continuation or positively autocorrelated effects exhibited over shorter time horizons shown by, among others, Lo and MacKinlay (1988). The explanation for the substantial amount of price reversal is based in behavior, in that investors tend to overweight recent performance and underweight longer-term or baseline information in their decisions.

For example, if a stock has recently suffered an earnings shortfall because of some temporary nonstructural shift in economic opportunities, the price decline may be exaggerated due to the recentness of the news. Once depressed, the price may be slow to recover until investors realize their "overreaction" to the temporary bad news associated with the earnings deficiency, which then creates buying pressure to "reverse" the price decline. Adjusting beliefs to realistic longer-term opportunities, instead of shorter-term prospects and bases of information, causes the reversal. DeBondt and Thaler (1985) find a significant persistence to this reversal phenomenon and indicate that markets tend to suffer from investor overreaction.

The beauty in DeBondt and Thaler is how simply an overreaction hypothesis can be tested empirically. Granted, there are always problems with experimental design, but their investigation is very straightforward and can be easily carried out using SAS.

Specifically, what DeBondt and Thaler do is calculate portfolio returns for some formation period—i.e., previous 36-month performance—and then see how that particular portfolio performs in an evaluation period—i.e., subsequent 36-month performance. To test the overreaction hypothesis, DeBondt and Thaler form loser and winner portfolios composed of the 30 worst-performing and 30 best-performing stocks, respectively, over the formation period. They then follow these portfolios for the subsequent 36 months and evaluate and compare their performance. Through time, the loser portfolio, made up of the worst-performing stocks in the formation period, consistently outperforms the winner portfolio during the evaluation period. These results, according to DeBondt and Thaler (1985), present strong evidence of stock market overreaction.

The purpose of this chapter is to show how simply you can carry out a straightforward stock market overreaction study. The SAS program code in this chapter also provides you with a few tricks for manipulating data.

Data Used for Analysis

DeBondt and Thaler (1985) cumulate market-adjusted returns over a three-year formation period for each New York Stock Exchange (NYSE) stock found on CRSP beginning in December 1932 and continuing through December 1977. The loser and winner portfolios are then evaluated over the 17 nonoverlapping three-year evaluation periods within that time period. Conrad and Kaul (1993) introduce the idea that cumulating returns over long horizons biases overreaction results. One suggested remedy is to use holding period returns when investigating long horizons. Hence, in this exercise, we use three-year holding period returns, instead of cumulative returns, for stocks listed on the NYSE, AMEX, and NASDAQ and found on the 1998 monthly CRSP tapes. The time period covered is from June 1929 through June 1998. Portfolios are evaluated over June-to-May periods. The return generation techniques and time periods used here are different from DeBondt and Thaler's. Quantitative differences result, but the exercise produces the same qualitative implications: loser portfolios dramatically outperform winner portfolios.

Sample SAS Code Evaluating the Existence of Return Reversals

Reading the Data

As with most research in financial economics, the first step taken to analyze data in SAS is to read observations from an external data set. This task is accomplished in the following data step.

Code 3.1: Read returns into SAS data set

```
data crspin; /*returns from crsp*/
     infile 'C:\contrary.output';
     input cusip $ yyyymmdd formret evalret;
     label formret = "Formation Return, 3yrs prior"
           evalret = "Evaluation Return, 3yrs hence";
     if formret > -1;
     if evalret > -1;
```

The last two statements in the data step are called *subsetting IFs*. These particular statements are used to include only data with valid returns. The variable definitions are as follows:

```
CUSIP        Firm-specific CUSIP identifier
YYYYMMDD     Date value identifier
FORMRET      Formation holding period return covering three years prior to
             the formation date
EVALRET      Evaluation holding period return covering three years
             subsequent to the formation date
```

Because the investigation of return reversal hinges on whether a portfolio changes course regarding performance, a specific date and time must be used as a starting point to form portfolios. The data read are firm-specific information, so all observations must be in date order before portfolio formation is accomplished. Not only does the data set have to be sorted by date, but sorting by returns also has to be accomplished. The easiest way to ensure proper date sequencing is to use PROC SORT. A quick illustration of the procedure is shown next.

Code 3.2: Sort returns by date and return performance

```
proc sort data=crspin;
     by yyyymmdd formret;
```

The effect of this step is that the data set is sorted by date of portfolio formation, and within each portfolio formation period the firms are sorted by return performance. By default, the sort sequence is from lowest to highest, or in return performance parlance, from the worst losers to the best winners.

Arranging the Data

The next PROC MEANS step calculates the number of firms in each portfolio formation period. We will need this counter later in the program.

Code 3.3: Count portfolio firms for each date

```
proc means data=crspin noprint;
    by yyyymmdd;
    var formret;
    output out=firms n = firmcnt;
```

In this step, we do not use PROC MEANS to compute descriptive statistics. Rather, it produces observation counts that are saved in a new data set, FIRMS. The OUTPUT statement, used in conjunction with the BY statement, instructs SAS to create one observation for each BY group (in this case, dates). Each record in FIRMS contains the number of firms that had valid return data within each portfolio formation period. We are required to do this step because each data portfolio formation period contains a different number of firms from which to choose the top and bottom performers.

To select only those loser and winner firms of interest, however, we must do some counting to determine the ranking of each firm and to determine how many firms are in each portfolio formation period. This counting is done in the next data step.

Code 3.4: Divide firms into winners and losers

```
data loser winner;
    merge crspin firms;
    by yyyymmdd;
    if first.yyyymmdd then firm=0;
    firm + 1;
    if firm <= 30 then output loser;
    if firm >= (firmcnt-29) then output winner;
```

Two useful SAS techniques are introduced in Code 3.4. First, the DATA step creates two new data sets, LOSER and WINNER. The LOSER data set contains the observations for all the "losing" firms, defined to be those firms with the poorest portfolio formation returns, whereas the WINNER data set contains those firms with the highest portfolio formation returns. You can use this multiple data set naming convention when separating data into different partitions.

The second technique introduced is *match merging*, which is illustrated with the MERGE CRSPIN FIRMS; BY YYYYMMDD; statements. The MERGE statement tells SAS to merge observations from the first data set (CRSPIN in this case) with the second data set, which is FIRMS. The BY YYYYMMDD; statement tells SAS to *match* observations from the second data set to the variable YYYYMMDD in the first data set. These statements generate a data series that has all the original variables read from the original data set (CRSPIN), along with the addition of the summary variables data set generated by PROC MEANS in Code 3.3. They also create the automatic SAS variables FIRST.YYYYMMDD and LAST.YYYYMMDD (these variables are created whenever a BY statement is used in a DATA step). These variables are indicators for the beginning and ending, respectively, of each set of records with identical values of YYYYMMDD. In the example above, we use FIRST.YYYYMMDD to reset the FIRM counter for each date group.

Having the two data sets merged by portfolio formation date is important when choosing how firms are classified into losers and winners. In this case, we take the bottom 30 and top 30 performers in each portfolio formation period. The counter FIRM is the selection variable that indicates which observations are then OUTPUT to the LOSER and WINNER data sets. Note that we initialize FIRM to zero; then the following statement, FIRM + 1, adds one and implicitly instructs the DATA step to make this value available to the next iteration (that is, reading the next observation).[1]

Analysis

After classifying firms as losers or winners, simple statistical averages for each portfolio must be calculated over the evaluation or subsequent time period to check for the existence of overreaction. If overreaction exists in the stock market, then you should expect that both portfolios experience price reversals. Simply, the loser portfolio in the formation period becomes the winner portfolio in the evaluation period, while the winner portfolio becomes a loser, or at minimum an underperforming portfolio in the evaluation period. In any case, the existence of overreactive security markets indicates that the loser portfolio, as defined by its performance in the preformation period, will outperform the winner portfolio in the evaluation period. Each portfolio's performance is now estimated with PROC MEANS.

Code 3.5: Compute returns and tests for past winner and loser portfolios

```
proc means data=loser n mean min max t prt;
    title 'Subsequent returns of loser portfolio';
    var evalret;
proc means data=winner n mean min max t prt;
    title 'Subsequent returns of winner portfolio';
    var evalret;
```

---

[1] FIRM +1 is, in fact, a shortcut for the following two statements: FIRM = FIRM+1; RETAIN FIRM;.

We use a TITLE statement to identify the results in the output. In addition to the number of observations, the mean, the minimum, and the maximum, the procedure is instructed to generate *t*-statistics and the corresponding significance levels (the T and PRT options, respectively). The following output is produced.

Output 3.1: The performance of past winner and loser portfolios

```
                    Subsequent returns of loser portfolio
                           The MEANS Procedure

           Analysis Variable : evalret Evaluation Return, 3yrs hence

    N          Mean           Minimum          Maximum    t Value    Pr > |t|
  2010     0.9774812       -0.9968750       88.9999770      12.44      <.0001

                    Subsequent returns of winner portfolio
                           The MEANS Procedure

           Analysis Variable : evalret Evaluation Return, 3yrs hence

    N          Mean           Minimum          Maximum    t Value    Pr > |t|
  2010     0.3920692       -0.9930350       14.6526070      13.57      <.0001
```

We find that the the loser portfolio returned an average 98% three-year holding period return after generating rock-bottom three-year performances in the prior portfolio formation periods. The winner portfolio, on the other hand, generated less than half the returns—approximately 40%—of the loser portfolio. Although the winner portfolios' performances may not be classified as subpar, or necessarily loser status, it is obvious that their previous outstanding performances were unsustainable. The *t*-statistics indicate that both means are significantly different from zero.

Summary

The purpose of this chapter was to show how SAS can be used to test the simple concept of return reversals in the stock market. The code used in this chapter's example can be easily modified to account for additional definitions of loser and winner portfolio descriptions. We leave it as an exercise for the reader to change loser and winner definitions to evaluate the sensitivity of overreaction strategies to time horizons.

Overreaction in the stock market may be a symptom of behavioral or psychological effects impacting market activities. Assuming that loser and winner portfolios do not differ systematically in other characteristics that determine returns, the simple test above is difficult to reconcile with the notion of a *homo economicus.*

Program Listing

```
data crspin; /*returns from crsp*/
    infile 'C:\contrary.output';
    input cusip $ yyyymmdd formret evalret;
    label formret = "Formation Return, 3yrs prior"
          evalret = "Evaluation Return, 3yrs hence";
    if formret > -1;
    if evalret > -1;

proc sort data=crspin;
    by yyyymmdd formret;
proc means data=crspin noprint;
    by yyyymmdd;
    var formret;
    output out=firms n = firmcnt;

data loser winner;
    merge crspin firms;
    by yyyymmdd;
    if first.yyyymmdd then firm=0;
    firm+1;
    if firm <=30 then output loser;
    if firm >= (firmcnt-29) then output winner;

proc means data=loser n mean min max t prt;
    title 'Subsequent returns of loser portfolio';
    var evalret;
proc means data=winner n mean min max t prt;
    title 'Subsequent returns of winner portfolio';
    var evalret;
run;
```

CHAPTER 4

CROSS-SECTIONAL APPROACH TO THE EMPIRICAL TEST OF THE CAPITAL ASSET PRICING MODEL

Key Concepts
- CAPM test
- Test for ARCH effects and autocorrelation
- Fama-MacBeth approach

Data: Monthly stock returns

Background

The capital asset pricing model (CAPM) developed by Sharpe (1964), Lintner (1965), and Black (1972) defines the systematic risk of a risky asset in terms of the beta coefficient—i.e., the ratio of an asset's covariance with the market portfolio to the variance of the market portfolio. At the moment, the CAPM and its implications are probably the most intensively investigated research areas in modern finance. Numerous studies are focusing on directly testing the empirical validity of the CAPM. In addition, the implications of the CAPM are investigated in such areas as the profitability of investment strategies, portfolio performance, and the estimation of the cost of capital. Findings of these studies are actively applied by practitioners, especially investment professionals.

The risk–returns relationship as defined by the CAPM is as follows:

$$E(R_i) = R_f + \beta_i \left[E(R_m) - R_f \right] \tag{4.1}$$

where $E(R_i)$ is the expected return on the ith asset, R_f is a risk-free interest rate, $E(R_m)$ is the expected return on the market portfolio, and β_i is the measure of the systematic risk. The market portfolio is an efficient portfolio containing all possible assets.

A direct empirical implication of the CAPM is a linear relationship between expected stock returns and the market betas, which completely explain the cross-sectional differences in expected returns. This implication is usually tested by using the cross-sectional regression approach. Another way to test the CAPM is based on the fact that the CAPM also implies mean-variance efficiency of the market portolio. In this book, we focus on the cross-sectional approach. It can also be applied to multifactor models and to the investigation of the so-called stock market anomalies such as E/P ratio or firm-size anomalies (see also Chapter 9).

The cross-sectional regression approach to testing the CAPM is usually implemented in two stages. First, estimates of the systematic risk (betas) are obtained by regressing each stock's returns on the market returns in time-series regressions. This estimation is known as the market model.

$$R_{it} = \alpha_i + \beta_i R_{mt} + \varepsilon_{it} \tag{4.2}$$

where α_i is a constant term, β_i is the market beta of the ith stock, R_{mt} is the market return, and ε_{it} is an error term. In the second stage, stock returns are regressed on the estimates of the market betas $\hat{\beta}_i$ from equation (4.2) in cross-sectional regressions:

$$R_i = \lambda_0 + \lambda_1 \hat{\beta}_i + \upsilon_i \tag{4.3}$$

where λ_0 is a constant term, λ_1 is the estimated slope coefficient, $\hat{\beta}_i$ is the market beta of the ith stock estimated by using equation (4.2), and υ_i is an error term.

One approach to the estimate in equation (4.3) is to first calculate the mean return for each stock over the sample period, and then regress the mean returns on the market betas estimated over the sample period. This approach is problematic, however, since stock returns are often cross-sectionally correlated and heteroscedastic. Results based on this approach can thus be misleading.

Fama and MacBeth (1973) suggest a much more sophisticated approach to testing the CAPM. They first estimate the cross-sectional regression in equation (4.3) for each month in the sample period and compute the sample mean of the estimated slope coefficients (the risk premiums associated with the market beta). Then they proceed to testing whether the average monthly slope coefficient is significantly different from zero. Shanken (1992) argues that ordinary least squares (OLS) estimates can be used because the cross-sectional estimates are not heteroscedastic. In this approach, the market betas to be used in each monthly cross-sectional regressions are usually estimated using data from the period preceding each month and are referred to as "rolling" betas.

Modifications of the basic two-staged testing procedure are also introduced in the literature. For instance, the betas can first be estimated for individual stocks and then for portfolios formed on the basis of the betas of individual stocks. The portfolio betas are then used in the cross-sectional regression. This approach aims to minimize the estimation errors in betas. In our example, we will use the basic Fama-MacBeth approach to illustrate the procedure.

The Data

The sample data are retrieved from CRSP and include all Standard & Poor's (S&P) 500 Index firms from 1979 to 1998. Stock prices are adjusted for stock splits and other distributions.

Sample SAS Code

Why Are SAS Macros Helpful?

The use of rolling betas in the cross-sectional regressions to test the CAPM requires a lot of repetitive calculations. The market model betas are estimated by "rolling" the estimation period by one month after previous estimation. Consequently, cross-sectional regressions are estimated for each month. Therefore, a SAS program that contains a single routine for all required estimations that could then be repeated as many times as needed would be very useful. This can be accomplished with the SAS macro facility, which we introduce in this chapter (the appendix summarizes the basic syntax of the SAS macro facility; also see Chapter 6 for an additional macro application).

Reading the Data

First, we read the stock return data from a text file into a SAS data set.

Code 4.1: Read the data

```
data aaa;
    infile 'c:\scapm_dem.dat';
    input firm $ date  yymmdd6. r rm;
    format date yymmdd6.;
```

In the data step, the monthly stock and market returns are read to the data set AAA from the external file 'CAPM.DAT'. We use the following variables:

```
FIRM  Firm identifier (CUSIP code)
DATE  Stock price date entered as yymmdd
R     Stock return
RM    Return on the S&P500 index
```

An important tool in SAS is informats and formats. An informat instructs the DATA step how to interpret a variable that it reads from an external file, such as the text file in our example. Note that we use the INPUT modifier YYMMDD6. following the variable DATE. This causes SAS to regard this variable as a six-digit date value, and especially to store it internally as a SAS date value. It is generally a good idea to store all dates (and times) using the SAS date and time values; among other advantages this allows, for example, arithmetic operations on dates. Consider the two hypothetical variables STARTDATE and ENDDATE, which have the values 971130 and 971201, respectively. If they are stored as SAS date values, then the difference DURATION = ENDDATE − STARTDATE would give the desired result of 1 day. When they are stored as numeric variables, the arithmetic difference is 71—and usually not what we would like to compute.

SAS date values are internally stored as integers (calculated as the number of days since January 1, 1960). To display SAS data values as actual dates when looking at data sets or at output, a FORMAT statement is necessary. In this case, we choose to display the dates the same way we originally entered them in the text file, but SAS allows several different date and time formats. Note also that the YYMMDD6. format takes into account century changes. This is achieved by the SAS system option YEARCUTOFF, which defaults to the value 30. This implies that SAS interprets year values between 0 and 30 as more recent than year values between 31 and 99.

Statistical Issues in Beta Estimation

The market model as described in equation (4.2) is estimated using a univariate regression model. Before we turn to the empirical tests of the CAPM, we briefly discuss how SAS can be used to verify the crucial OLS assumptions. Typical violations of these assumptions include autocorrelated and heteroscedastic disturbance terms.

The correlation between any two disturbances should be zero. If this assumption does not hold, the disturbances are said to be autocorrelated. Heteroscedasticity occurs if the variance of the disturbance term is not constant (see, e.g., Judge et al. (1985) for an in-depth econometric discussion of the OLS assumptions).[1]

---

[1] G. G. Judge, W. E. Griffiths, R. C. Hill, H. Luetkepohl, and T. C. Lee, *The Theory and Practice of Econometrics*, 2d ed. (New York: Wiley, 1985).

Next, we estimate the market model betas for a single stock and test for autocorrelation and heteroscedasticity using PROC AUTOREG. The WHERE data set option selects one firm and only dates before May 5, 1988. Note also that we use the MDY function in the statement. This function converts numeric values to SAS date values; this conversion is necessary because only variables of identical types can be compared (and the variable DATE is also a SAS date value). This procedure can also be used to correct for the autocorrelation and heteroscedasticity.

Code 4.2: Estimate market model and specification tests for a single stock

```
PROC AUTOREG DATA = aaa (where=(firm='00811710' and date<=mdy(05,05,88)));
    model r = rm / archtest dw=4 dwprob;
quit;
```

The MODEL statement defines the regression of stock returns on market returns. The option ARCHTEST prints the portmanteau and the Engle Lagrange multiplier test statistics to analyze conditional heteroscedasticity.[2] The DW=4 option prints the Durbin-Watson test statistic up to the fourth order, and DWPROB prints the corresponding probability values.

Output 4.1 shows the estimation results for a single stock. *Regress R-Square* refers to the explanatory power of the model, which equals 0.1991. The *Durbin-Watson statistic* for the first-order autocorrelation of the residuals and the generalized Durbin-Watson statistics for the higher orders are printed in the second section of the output. Pr<DW is the *p*-value for testing positive autocorrelation, and Pr>DW is the *p*-value for testing negative autocorrelation. The results indicate no significant autocorrelation up to the fourth lag.

The portmanteau *Q* test statistics and the Engle Lagrange multiplier test (LM test) for heteroscedasticity are printed in the third section of the output. Probability values associated with the test statistics are insignificant, indicating that the model is not conditionally heteroscedastic at lags 1 through 12.

The estimated regression parameters are printed at the end of the output. The estimated market model beta RM is 1.25437 ($p = 0.0012$), and the estimated intercept is −0.00461 ($p = 0.0173$).

---

[2] For a more in-depth analysis, not only with regard to heteroscedasticity, PROC MODEL provides more flexibility, but also more complexity.

Output 4.1: Market model and specification tests for one stock

```
                        The AUTOREG Procedure
                      Dependent Variable      r

                    Ordinary Least Squares Estimates

        SSE                    0.00753689    DFE                      48
        MSE                    0.0001570     Root MSE            0.01253
        SBC                    -290.2805     AIC              -294.10455
        Regress R-Square          0.1991     Total R-Square       0.1991

                      Durbin-Watson Statistics

            Order            DW      Pr < DW    Pr > DW
              1           1.9994      0.4931     0.5069
              2           1.8407      0.3338     0.6662
              3           2.0667      0.7027     0.2973
              4           1.9639      0.6210     0.3790
NOTE: Pr<DW is the p-value for testing positive autocorrelation, and Pr>DW
      is the p-value for testing negative autocorrelation.

                    Q and LM Tests for ARCH Disturbances

          Order          Q      Pr > Q          LM      Pr > LM

            1         0.0886     0.7659       0.0110     0.9166
            2         0.4744     0.7888       0.0486     0.9760
            3         0.4980     0.9193       0.3200     0.9562
            4         0.7166     0.9493       0.9512     0.9171
            5         0.8904     0.9709       1.3933     0.9250
            6         0.9761     0.9865       1.6578     0.9483
            7         0.9811     0.9951       1.6965     0.9747
            8         1.3046     0.9955       2.3658     0.9677
            9         1.3057     0.9983       2.4441     0.9823
           10         1.4560     0.9991       2.7952     0.9858
           11         1.5636     0.9995       3.1262     0.9890
           12         1.8047     0.9997       3.5456     0.9903

                                    Standard              Approx
        Variable    DF     Estimate     Error   t Value   Pr > |t|
        Intercept    1    -0.004610   0.001870    -2.47     0.0173
        rm           1     1.2544     0.3632       3.45     0.0012
```

Cross-Sectional Regression Method to Testing the CAPM

Before we can start implementing the Fama-MacBeth approach and estimate the market model betas, we have to construct the time series of stock returns for each firm. First, we determine the beginning and ending dates of the return series for each firm.

Code 4.3: Define beginning and end of the time series of stock returns for each firm

```
proc sort data=aaa;
    by firm date;

data begin (keep=firm bgndate) end (keep=firm enddate);
    set aaa;
    by firm;
    if first.firm then do;
            bgndate=date;
            format bgndate yymmdd6.;
            output begin;
    end;
    if last.firm then do;
            enddate=date;
            format enddate yymmdd6.;
            output end;
    end;
```

After the data are sorted by firm and date, the DATA step creates two new data sets: BEGIN and END. The KEEP data set option instructs SAS to write only two variables to each of them, the firm identifier and a date variable that we compute below. Note that we use the BY statement in the DATA step. Whenever it appears in a DATA step, SAS creates two automatic variables that are named FIRST.VARIABLE and LAST.VARIABLE, where VARIABLE is the name following the BY statement. These are indicator variables; the former assumes a value of unity only for the first observation of a BY group, and the latter a value of unity only for the last observation. For all other observations they contain zeros. Here, we use these indicators to find the first and last observation for each firm. For example, when FIRST.FIRM is not equal to zero, the current date is the first return date for the firm. It is assigned to the variable BGNDATE, assigned a SAS date format, and written to the output data set BEGIN. Then we proceed accordingly for the last date of each firm. Each of the output data sets now contains one observation per firm indicating the beginning and ending dates, respectively, of the return time series.

Next, we would like to identify firms that do not have a sufficiently long time series of returns available. To do that, we first merge the begin and end data sets.

Code 4.4: Identify firms for which the required time series of returns is available

```
data length;
    merge begin end;
    by firm;
    * delete firms with too few return days;
    if bgndate > mdy(02,25,88) then delete;
    if enddate < mdy(05,31,88) then delete;
    keep firm;
```

The subsetting IF statements are used to exclude firms for which the full time series of stock returns is not available. The data set LENGTH again has one observation per firm, but only for those firms for which the return series is of sufficient length. Next, this information is combined with the raw data we read in to data set AAA earlier.

Code 4.5: Exclude firms for which the required time series of returns is not available

```
data gooddata;
    merge aaa length (in=a);
    by firm;
    if a;
    n + 1;
    if first.firm then n=1;
```

We write records to the new data set GOODDATA only if the firm is listed in the LENGTH data set. This is accomplished with the data set option IN, which creates an indicator variable A that has a value of one whenever a record is read from the data set LENGTH. We then use a subsetting IF statement to select only records where A is not zero. This procedure creates a returns data set GOODDATA that contains only returns from firms that were not deleted from LENGTH in the previous DATA step. Finally, the statement *n* +1 creates a variable to count the observations in the time series of stock returns for each firm. It is reset to one whenever the first observation of a new firm is found.

Next, we use the macro ESTIM to estimate rolling betas for each stock in the sample. SAS macros are used to generate the text for a SAS program that is subsequently executed. We provide a short summary of macro statements in the appendix to this chapter, and a more comprehensive application in Chapter 6. You can view the generated statements in the system log by specifying OPTIONS MPRINT (as with all commands, followed by a semicolon) at the beginning of the program.

Code 4.6: Macro to estimate rolling betas of individual stocks

```
%macro estim;
%do x = 50 %to 66;
    data temp;
            set gooddata;
            if &x - 49 <= n <= &x;
            per =  &x;
        proc reg data = temp noprint outest = results;
            model r = rm;
            by firm per;
            quit;
        proc append base = betas1 data = results;
%end;
%mend estim;
%estim

data betas2;
    set betas1;
    n = per + 1;
    alpha = intercept;
    beta = rm;
    keep firm n alpha beta;
```

We choose to estimate the betas over 50 months. The main tasks of this macro are enclosed in a %DO loop that executes them 17 times, letting the macro variable X vary from 50 to 66 in increments of one. All estimations are based on the new data set TEMP. Because the rolling betas are estimated from different time series in each iteration loop, its contents must change for each iteration. This is achieved by the statement IF &x-49 <= n <= &x. The variable N, created in Code 4.5, identifies each observation in the time series of stock returns for a given firm, and the macro variable X is defined in the enclosing %DO loop. Thus, the IF statement subsets the original data such that the correct time series of returns is used in each iteration loop. The following example shows the IF statements generated by ESTIM as the value of the variable X changes in every iteration loop:

```
&x      IF &x-49 <= n <= &x

50      IF 1 <= n <= 50
51      IF 2 <= n <= 51
        IF 3 <= n <= 52

...
```

In the first iteration, the variable X has a value of 50 and the IF statement restricts the data such that only the observations from 1 to 50 in the time series of returns of each stock are used in the estimations. In the second iteration loop, the observations from 2 to 51 in the time series of stock returns are used, and so on.

To estimate the betas for each stock and each period, we use PROC REG based on equation (4.2) and write the regression estimates to the new data set RESULTS.[3] Note the use of the new variable PER to indicate the last observation in the time series of returns used in the estimation. The BY FIRM PER statement ensures that PER is saved in the data set RESULTS; we will need it later to match the estimated betas with the original data before we can estimate the cross-sectional regressions.

The OUTPUT option would overwrite the existing data set in each iteration; to avoid this, we have to create a new data set and in each iteration add the regression output to it. This is achieved by PROC APPEND, which creates a new data set BETAS1 in the first iteration and subsequently adds each individual regression output. Then the %DO loop is closed by a corresponding %END statement, and the %MEND statement marks the end of the macro definition. Finally, the %ESTIM statement executes the macro.

The subsequent DATA step is then used to give more intuitive names to the estimated market model parameters. The variable ALPHA refers to the estimated alpha, and the variable BETA refers to the estimated betas. A new variable N indicates the first month after each beta estimation period ends. This information is needed when the betas and alphas are matched with the return data from the next month to estimate the cross-sectional regressions.

Next, we need to combine the original return data with the estimated market model coefficients so we can estimate the effect of alphas and betas on subsequent returns. PROC SORT is used to sort the estimated coefficients by firms and period. Then a MERGE statement combines the return data in GOODDATA and the regression coefficients in BETAS2 using firms and periods as merge keys. The statement IF BETA ^=. (alternatively, IF BETA NE.) restricts the cross-sectional regressions to periods when estimated market model betas are available. Note that by construction, market model estimates are not available for the first 50 months of the data.

Code 4.7: Combine data and estimate cross-sectional regressions of return on beta

```
proc sort data = betas2;
    by firm n;
data fmb;
    merge gooddata betas2;
    by firm n;
    if beta ^=.;
proc sort data = fmb;
    by date;
proc reg data=fmb noprint outest = final;
    model r = beta;
    by date;
quit;
proc means mean n std t prt data = final;
    var intercept beta;
```

---

[3] Alternatively, we could use PROC AUTOREG to generate betas. We present the example using PROC REG because, due to its greater flexibility, this procedure is likely to be used by most researchers for this purpose.

PROC REG then estimates the cross-sectional regressions as described in equation (4.3). Monthly returns are regressed on the market model betas estimated over the period that ends in the preceding month. These cross-sectional regressions are repeated for each month (the BY DATE statement), and the estimated coefficients are written to the data set FINAL. To summarize the estimates, PROC MEANS computes the time-series averages of the intercepts and betas from the cross-sectional regressions.

Output 4.2: Cross-sectional regressions of returns on beta

```
                        The MEANS Procedure

Variable   Label                Mean    N     Std Dev  t Value  Pr > |t|
Intercept  Intercept       0.0040615   17   0.0221914     0.75    0.4614
beta                     -0.000617107   17   0.0121632    -0.21    0.8369
```

The corresponding output contains the results of testing the CAPM using the rolling beta approach. The average slope estimate (the lambda in equation 4.3) is not significantly different from zero ($p = 0.8369$). Thus, actual returns appear to have no significant relation to the CAPM beta, and we cannot reject the null hypothesis that the CAPM does not explain returns.

Program Listing

```
data aaa;
    infile 'c:\capm_dem.dat';
    input firm $ date  yymmdd6. r rm;
    format date yymmdd6.;

proc autoreg data = aaa (where=(firm='00811710' and date<=mdy(05,05,88)));
    model r = rm / archtest dw=4 dwprob;
quit;

proc sort data=aaa;
by firm date;

data begin (keep=firm bgndate) end (keep=firm enddate);
    set aaa;
    by firm;
    if first.firm then do;
        bgndate=date;
        format bgndate yymmdd6.;
        output begin;
    end;
```

```
if last.firm then do;
            enddate=date;
            format enddate yymmdd6.;
            output end;
    end;

data length;
    merge begin end;
    by firm;
    * delete firms with too few return days;
    if bgndate > mdy(02,25,88) then delete;
    if enddate < mdy(05,31,88) then delete;
    keep firm;

data gooddata;
    merge aaa length (in=a);
    by firm;
    if a;
    n + 1;
    if first.firm then n=1;

%macro estim;
%do x = 50 %to 66;
    data temp;
            set gooddata;
            if &x - 49 <= n <= &x;
            per =  &x;
    proc reg data = temp noprint outest = results;
            model r = rm;
            by firm per;
            quit;
    proc append base = betas1 data = results;
%end;
%mend estim;
%estim

data betas2;
    set betas1;
    n = per + 1;
    alpha = intercept;
    beta = rm;
    keep firm n alpha beta;

proc sort data = betas2;
    by firm n;

data fmb;
    merge gooddata betas2;
    by firm n;
    if beta ^=.;
```

```
proc sort data = fmb;
    by date;

proc reg data=fmb noprint outest = final;
    model r = beta;
    by date;
quit;

proc means mean n std t prt data = final;
    var intercept beta;

run;
```

Appendix: A Short Introduction to SAS Macros

The SAS macro facility is a powerful tool for reducing the amount of code you have to write in your programs and for customizing SAS. This can save much time and make programs easier to read in cases like the previous CAPM example. You can use the macro facility in two basic ways: by using macro variables or by using macros. A macro variable is a text variable that has only a single value, and such variables can be used anywhere in a program. It is not necessary to define a macro in order to use a macro variable, and its value can be any text that you would like to use in the program. The simplest way to define and assign values to a macro variable is to use the %LET statement as follows:

```
%LET name = John;
```

Note that you do not have to use quotation marks around the value of the macro variable—the content is always a text string. You can now use the macro variable NAME in any part of your SAS code to refer to the name "John." All you have to do is to place an ampersand (&) in front of the name of the macro variable and add the macro variable into your code. You can then use it, for example, in TITLE statements:

```
TITLE = "&name is a good fellow";
```

Note the use of the double quotation marks. They are needed because the macro processor resolves references to macro variables only in double quotes.

Now, if you know other good fellows in addition to John, you can simply assign their names to the macro variable *name* in the %LET statement. This saves time, because you do not have to rewrite each part of the code where you refer to good fellows. All you have to do is to edit a single %LET statement. This also comes in handy if, for example, a program repeatedly refers to the same long list of variables.

The previous example is a very simple illustration of the advantages the SAS macro facility provides. A macro is a piece of SAS code that can be used repeatedly within a SAS program. The simplest macros are much like macro variables, but macros can also do very complicated tasks (see the event study program in Chapter 6). In its most basic form, a macro is a piece of SAS code placed between the %MACRO and %MEND statements, as shown here:

```
%MACRO example;
     < SAS-code>
%MEND example;
```

The %MACRO EXAMPLE statement tells SAS where the definition of the macro EXAMPLE starts, and %MEND EXAMPLE tells where it ends. The SAS code between the %MACRO and %MEND statements defines what the macro actually does. After a macro has been compiled (SAS, by default, does this automatically before any other statements are executed), it can be invoked anywhere in the program simply by adding a percent sign (%) to the beginning of its name:

```
%example
```

Note that a macro invocation is the only instance when no semicolon is necessary to complete a SAS command. The reason is that a terminating semicolon is already contained in the code within the macro. The invocation replaces the %EXAMPLE statement with the code contained in the macro.

Macros have a simple structure, but they can be very versatile. For example, they can be nested or invoked within another macro. Parameters can be passed to the statements within a macro and allow more control over the execution of a macro. For instance, you can change the data that the macro is using (see Chapter 6).

Macro program statements always start with a percent sign and control the execution of a macro. It is important to understand the difference between macro and SAS statements: the former are only available inside the macro, while the latter are later executed after the macro has been compiled. Typically, macro statements are used to create conditional or repeated SAS statements. Frequently used macro program statements include the following:

```
%GLOBAL
```

Creates a global macro variable, that is, a macro variable that can be used anywhere in the program—both inside and outside a macro.

```
%LET
```

Creates a macro variable and assigns it a value or changes the value of an existing macro variable.

```
%DO...%END
```

Statements following the %DO statements are treated as a unit until a matching %END statement appears.

```
%DO...%TO...%END
```

Statements following the %DO...%TO statement are repeated as many times as indicated by the value of a macro variable used as an index variable.

An example of a frequently used macro function is

```
%EVAL(expression)
```

This function evaluates arithmetic and logical expressions. Note that the %EVAL function does not allow calculations in fractions—that is, variables in *expressions* can have only integer values. If a division operation results in a fraction, the fraction is truncated to an integer.

CHAPTER 5

EVENT STUDIES

Key Concepts
- Market model regression
- Abnormal returns

Data Concepts
- Daily stock returns
- Quarterly earnings
- Quarterly earnings announcement date

Background

Event studies constitute a large area of research investigating the stock market response to public announcements of new value-relevant information. Typically, stock return behavior is analyzed in a relative short period of time, such as a few days surrounding the announcement date. The more precisely the announcement date can be measured, the more powerful and reliable the analysis. Event studies have been applied to numerous types of events. Stock splits, mergers, and earnings announcements are typical examples of events investigated in this literature. The direct implication of the market efficiency hypothesis for event studies is that prices should reflect all the new information without delay when it arrives in the market. The event study of stock splits by Fama et al. (1969) is often referred to as one of the pioneering works in the area. Ball and Brown (1968) launched a whole literature investigating stock price reactions to the announcements of earnings.

The typical event study is designed in the following way. First, we need to obtain precise announcement dates for a sample of firms. At this stage, it is important to make sure that no other announcements are close to the ones that are investigated. Their confounding effect would contaminate the estimates of the price reactions to the event of interest. After a clean sample of events is obtained in this way, the next step is to collect daily returns for the sample firms and also to use an appropriate market index. A reasonable length for the period would be, for example, from 244 days before to five days after the event. This period would have 250 daily observations.

Next, we define an estimation period for estimating the market model. This period needs to be sufficiently long to allow efficient estimates; most researchers choose around 200 trading days prior to the event. It is important to ascertain that the estimation period is free of any effects related to the events that are investigated. For example, it is well known that acquisition targets experience substantial price increases during the 20 trading days preceding the actual announcement. In such cases, estimation should end a few weeks before the announcement (for example, it could run from day –250 to day –20 relative to the announcement). Then a market model is estimated for each firm during this period by regressing firm-specific returns on contemporaneous market returns. The estimated intercepts and slope coefficients are recorded.

We use the estimated coefficients to compute expected returns during an event period (when we expect the stock price to react to the event). If markets are efficient with respect to public information, we expect that the new information is quickly impounded into stock prices; this typically happens within a few minutes. Therefore, a one-day event period that includes the announcement day only (day 0) is the best choice if the announcement date is known exactly. In practice, however, we may not be able to pinpoint precisely the time when the new information reaches investors. As previously mentioned, it is well known that mergers are preceded by substantial stock-price "run-ups" prior to the announcement—this could be caused by insider trading or public speculation about the upcoming transaction. Thus, there is a trade-off: if the event window is too short, it may not include the time when investors truly learn about the event; if it is too long, other information (which flows constantly) will make the statistical detection harder and less reliable. For most purposes, an event window that includes the event day and the prior day should be sufficient. If pre-event leakage is suspected, we might also analyze windows that extend further back in time, such as (–5,0) or (–10,0) event periods. Generally, the event period should not extend more than one day beyond the announcement, or else unrelated information can too easily affect the results.

Measuring Abnormal Stock Returns

Stock returns move in response to several firm or market-specific factors. The key issue in event studies is what portion of the price movement is actually caused by the event of interest. In other words, we have to extract the impact of the one particular event on stock returns from the total returns. This leads to the concept of abnormal returns. The abnormal return of the ith stock, AR_{it}, is obtained by subtracting the normal or expected return in the absence of the event, $E(R_{it})$, from the actual return in the event period, R_{it}:

$$AR_{it} = R_{it} - E(R_{it}) \tag{5.1}$$

There are several alternative ways to measure the expected returns in equation (5.1). Frequently used benchmarks for expected returns include the returns predicted by the market model, market returns, and firm-specific average returns from a past period. The market model is probably the most frequently used approach, and it will also be implemented in our SAS example.[1] The market model equation is expressed as follows:

$$R_{it} = \alpha_i + \beta_i R_{mt} + \varepsilon_{it}, \text{where } t = -250, \ldots, -11 \tag{5.2}$$

where α_i is a constant term for the ith stock, β_i is the market beta of the ith stock, R_{mt} is the market return, and ε_{it} is an error term. The parameters of the model are estimated by using the time-series data from the estimation period that precedes each individual announcement. The estimated parameters are then matched with the actual returns in the event period. Thus, the abnormal returns in equation (5.1) are calculated from actual returns during the event period and the estimated coefficients from the estimation period:

$$AR_{it} = R_{it} - \hat{\alpha}_i - \hat{\beta}_i R_{mt}, \text{where } t = -10, \ldots, +10 \tag{5.3}$$

The Data

The specific events examined in this portion of the text relate to earnings surprises, which are defined later. The data used in this chapter are from Compustat and CRSP for the period from 1979 to 1998. Specifically, we arbitrarily select 324 quarterly earnings announcement dates by 10 firms and the corresponding quarterly earnings from Compustat, and daily returns from CRSP. We also obtain the return on the equally weighted CRSP combined index.

In event studies, it is important to investigate the impact of the *unexpected* part of the new information on stock returns. This is because in efficient markets, stock prices already reflect the expected information, and only the unexpected part should have any impact on prices. Unexpected earnings are usually measured as a difference between the published earnings and the earnings forecasted by financial analysts. In our sample data, the unexpected earnings are simply measured as a difference between the earnings from quarters t and t-1. You can easily modify the sample code to use earnings forecasts in the calculation of the unexpected earnings.[2]

To shorten the discussion of the program, some of the important terms that will be used throughout the discussion are defined in the following list. Read these definitions very carefully!

---

[1] The market model is a single-factor model. Expected returns can also be modeled using multifactor models that contain, for example, macroeconomic variables in addition to the market return as explanatory variables (see, for instance, Chen et al., 1986).

[2] The change in quarterly earnings as a measure of unexpected earnings is problematic especially for those firms that have strong seasonal variation in earnings.

Announcement Date or Event Date

The first date when the public learns about the event (here, quarterly earnings) is termed the announcement date and we refer to it as day "0." The other days are expressed relative to the announcement date. Event study methodology crucially depends on accurate event dates—the more precisely the announcement date can be determined, the more powerful and reliable is the analysis.

Event Period

The event period surrounds the earnings announcement date during which the stock market response to the earnings announcement is investigated.

Event Period Abnormal Returns (ARs)

Market model abnormal stock returns are calculated for each day in the event period. The market model parameters are estimated from the estimation period. These parameters are then matched with the return data from the event period.

Cumulative Event Period Abnormal Returns (CARs)

CARs are abnormal daily returns cumulated over part of the event period.

Estimation Period

The estimation period must not be affected by the event and is used to estimate "normal" stock price behavior. It is very important that returns during this period not be affected by the event in any way.

Sample Program

Reading and Organizing the Data

As before, the SAS program for the event study is discussed in several parts. We start by reading the data.

Code 5.1: Read data on event dates and returns

```
* read data from text file;
data returns;
    infile 'c:\edata.dat';
    input firm $ @10 date yymmdd6. @17 evntdate yymmdd6. evntdum $ ret
mrktret;
    format date evntdate yymmdd6.;
    before = date < evntdate;
```

The data are read to the data set RETURNS from a text file, which contains 121 daily observations for each announcement (110 trading days before and 10 after the event date). We again use the informat YYMMDD6. to store dates as SAS date values. The FORMAT statement does not affect any computations, but it helps reading the dates when looking directly at the data. Note the use of line controls: the @10 control in front of the variable date, for example, instructs the DATA step to start looking for the date in column 10 of the input data set. When using formatted input, it is usually a good idea to also use line controls to make the input statement unambiguous. The following variables are used:

FIRM	Firm-specific CUSIP
DATE	Return date
EVNTDATE	Event date
EVNTDUM	A portfolio code that indicates whether the announced earnings were below/above the expected earnings.
RET	Daily stock return
MRKRET	Daily market return
BEFORE	This dummy variable has a one for all days before the event.

Next, we will create a variable that counts the trading days relative to the event date. For example, it should contain a zero for the event date itself, a –1 for the trading day before, and so on. This variable can then be used to compute averages across certain windows for different events. Because each firm may have a different number of trading days prior to the event, we first determine how many trading days we have available for each event.

Code 5.2: Determine the number of pre-event returns for each security

```
* sort and determine number of days with data before event date;
proc sort data=returns;
    by firm evntdate date;
proc means data=returns noprint;
    by firm evntdate;
    output out=nreturns(drop=_type_ _freq_) sum(before)= bef_sum;
```

Here, PROC MEANS creates a new data set NRETURNS that contains the number of pre-event trading days for each announcement. This variable is now merged with the original return data. Based on this variable, we can then create the date counter. To save disk space, it is usually a good idea to remove unneeded variables from data sets. Here, we remove the variables _TYPE_ and _FREQ_, which are automatically generated by PROC MEANS, because they are not used in the subsequent calculations.

Code 5.3: Divide the data into estimation and event period returns

```
* compute event date counter and split data into estimation and event
periods;
data estper evntper;
    merge returns(drop=before) nreturns;
    by firm evntdate;
    if first.evntdate then relday=-bef_sum - 1;
    relday + 1;
    if relday < -10 then output estper;
    if -1 <= relday <= 0 then output evntper;
```

Note that the MERGE statement merges each observation in RETURNS, which has several records per event, with each observation in NRETURNS, which has one record per event. As a result, the matching records from the latter are repeated for each daily return record. We use the BY statement in the DATA step to make the automatic variables available that indicate the beginning and end of each BY group. Here, whenever the first record for an event is read, the new variable RELDAY is set to the number of pre-event days (minus one, and the next line adds one again). This variable now contains the relative days we need to subset the estimation and event periods: ESTPER contains estimation period data (more than 10 trading days before the event), and EVNTPER contains the returns for days –1 and 0 relative to the event.

Estimating the Market Model Parameters

In this section, we use the estimation period data to estimate the market model for each announcement based on equation (5.2). The parameters are necessary to compute the abnormal returns later on.

Code 5.4: Estimate market model parameters

```
* compute market model parameters in estimation period;
proc reg data=estper outest=mmparam (rename=(intercept=alpha mrktret=beta)
    keep=firm evntdate intercept mrktret) noprint;
    by firm evntdate;
    model ret = mrktret;
quit;
```

PROC REG is used to estimate the market model regression separately for each firm–event date combination. The OUTEST option instructs PROC REG to write the estimated coefficients to the new data set MMPARAM. SAS names the estimates such that INTERCEPT refers to the intercept of the regression model, and the names of independent variables refer to the estimates of corresponding slope coefficients. The RENAME data set option changes these to more intuitive names. The KEEP data set option then instructs the procedure to write only the firm-event identifiers, the intercept coefficient, and the beta coefficient to the output data set. Note that although the renaming is done in the same step, the KEEP statement must use the old names and not the new ones. Finally, the NOPRINT option instructs the procedure not to print any results to the output screen.

The MODEL statement defines the regression equation. Since we are estimating the market model, the daily stock return (RET) is the dependent variable and the daily market return (MRKTRET) is the independent variable.

Calculating the Market Model Abnormal Stock Returns

In this section, we use the estimated market model coefficients to compute abnormal returns for each day in the event period.

Code 5.5: Compute abnormal returns

```
* compute abnormal returns in event period;
data ar;
    merge evntper mmparam;
    by firm evntdate;
    ar  = ret - alpha - beta * mrktret;

* compute cumulative abnormal returns;
proc means data=ar noprint;
    by firm evntdate;
    id evntdum;
    output out = car sum(ar)=car;
```

First, we have to merge the coefficients with the event-period data. The MERGE statement combines the estimated market model parameters in the data set MMPARAM (one observation per firm-event combination) with the daily stock returns for the event period in the data set EVNTPER (one observation *for each day in the event period* for each firm-event combination). The statement AR = RET - ALPHA - BETA * MRKTRET computes abnormal returns following equation (5.3).

Now we have a data set that contains abnormal returns for each announcement and each of the two days in the event period. To calculate cumulative abnormal returns we use PROC MEANS. The output statement in PROC MEANS writes the cumulative abnormal returns, CAR, to the new data set CAR. The keyword SUM(AR)=CAR instructs PROC MEANS to compute the sum of the abnormal returns AR and to name that sum CAR. Because the input data set contains only the days in the event period, these statements yield the cumulative abnormal returns over the event period.

Calculating the Abnormal Returns of Portfolios and Testing the Statistical Significance of the Results

In the last part of this example, we compute cumulative abnormal returns for the portfolios of positive and negative unexpected earnings. We also test whether the difference in the cumulative abnormal returns of the two portfolios is statistically significant.

Code 5.6: Calculating the abnormal returns of portfolios and testing the statistical significance of the results

```
* sort by portfolio type and output summary and test statistics;
proc sort data=car;
     by evntdum;
proc means data=car n mean t prt;
     title "overall results";
     var car;
proc means data=car n mean t prt;
     title "results by direction of earnings surprise";
     var car;
     by evntdum;
proc ttest data=car;
     title "test of equal AR for positive and negative earnings surprises";
     var car;
     class evntdum;
```

First, we sort the data by the variable EVNTDUM, because we would like to contrast differences between positive and negative earnings surprises. The first PROC MEANS statement computes the simple average CAR, the associated cross-sectional *t*-statistic, and the corresponding significance level (we discuss alternative tests in Chapter 6). The second PROC MEANS statement produces the same statistics separately for positive and negative surprises. Finally, PROC TTEST is used to test whether the cumulative abnormal returns of positive and negative surprises are different from each other. The results follow.

Output 5.1: Results of analyzing the cumulative abnormal returns of firms with positive and negative earnings surprises

```
                            Overall results
                          The MEANS Procedure
                        Analysis Variable : CAR


              N            Mean      t Value    Pr > |t|
            324         0.0017152      0.93      0.3547



              Results by direction of earnings surprise
       -------------------------- evntdum=1 --------------------------------
                        Analysis Variable : CAR


              N            Mean      t Value    Pr > |t|
            148        -0.0022430     -0.83      0.4104


       -------------------------- evntdum=2 --------------------------------
                        Analysis Variable : CAR


              N            Mean      t Value    Pr > |t|
            176         0.0050438      2.01      0.0457



       Test of equal AR for positive and negative earnings surprises
                          The TTEST Procedure
                             Statistics


                               Lower CL              Upper CL   Lower CL
Variable    evntdum        N     Mean     Mean         Mean     Std Dev    Std Dev
CAR         1            148    -0.008   -0.002       0.0031    0.0297     0.0331
CAR         2            176     0.0001   0.005        0.01     0.0301     0.0332
CAR         Diff (1-2)         -0.015   -0.007      -11E-6     0.0308     0.0332

                             Statistics
                             Upper CL
       Variable    evntdum    Std Dev    Std Err    Minimum    Maximum
       CAR         1          0.0373     0.0027     -0.091     0.1026
       CAR         2          0.0371     0.0025     -0.09      0.1264
       CAR         Diff (1-2) 0.0359     0.0037
```

Output 5.1 (continued)

```
                           T-Tests
Variable      Method          Variances      DF    t Value    Pr > |t|
CAR           Pooled          Equal          322    -1.97      0.0497
CAR           Satterthwaite   Unequal        313    -1.97      0.0496

                    Equality of Variances
     Variable      Method      Num DF    Den DF    F Value    Pr > F
     CAR           Folded F      175       147      1.01       0.9450
```

The overall results show that the average CAR is 0.17% and not statistically different from zero. When separated according to the direction of the earnings surprise, however, we find that positive surprises are associated with significantly positive CARs at a significance level of better than 5%. Finally, the *t*-test across the two portfolios is also significant: it rejects the null hypothesis of equal CARs across these groups at a significance level of 4.97%.

Program Listing

```
* read data from text file;
data returns;
    infile 'c:\edata.dat';
    input firm $ @10 date yymmdd6. @17 evntdate yymmdd6. evntdum $ ret
mrktret;
    format date evntdate yymmdd6.;
    before = date < evntdate;

* sort and determine number of days with data before event date;
proc sort data=returns;
    by firm evntdate date;
proc means data=returns noprint;
    by firm evntdate;
    output out=nrets(drop=_type_ _freq_) sum(before)= bef_sum;

* compute event date counter and split data into estimation and event
periods;
data estper evntper;
    merge returns(drop=before) nrets;
    by firm evntdate;
    if first.evntdate then relday=-bef_sum - 1;
    relday + 1;
    if relday < -10 then output estper;
    if -1 <= relday <= 0 then output evntper;
```

```
* compute market model parameters in estimation period;
proc reg data=estper outest=mmparam (rename=(intercept=alpha mrktret=beta)
keep=firm evntdate intercept mrktret) noprint;
    by firm evntdate;
    model ret = mrktret;
quit;

* compute abnormal returns in event period;
data ar;
    merge evntper mmparam;
    by firm evntdate;
    ar  = ret - alpha - beta * mrktret;

* compute cumulative abnormal returns;
proc means data=ar noprint;
    by firm evntdate;
    id evntdum;
    output out = car sum(ar)=car;

* sort by portfolio type and output summary and test statistics;
proc sort data=car;
    by evntdum;
proc means data=car n mean t prt;
    title "overall results";
    var car;
proc means data=car n mean t prt;
    title "results by direction of earnings surprise";
    var car;
    by evntdum;
proc ttest data=car;
    title "test of equal ar for positive and negative earnings surprises";
    var car;
    class evntdum;
run;
```

CHAPTER 6

EFFECTIVE USE OF SAS MACROS: AN APPLICATION TO EVENT STUDIES

Key Concepts
- Market model regression
- Abnormal returns
- Testing abnormal returns
- Effect of earnings surprises on returns

Data Concepts
- Daily stock returns
- Quarterly earnings
- Quarterly earnings announcement date

This chapter illustrates how SAS macros can be used to solve more complicated programming tasks in empirical research. We continue using an event study as the example, because most applications involve a significant number of repetitive estimations and calculations. We extend the event study program discussed in Chapter 5 by including more sophisticated test statistics and increasing the flexibility with the definition of the return window.

Alternative Test Statistics in Event Studies

There are numerous tests for evaluating the statistical significance of abnormal returns. Several studies have developed tests to control for specific problems that occur with event studies. Each tests the null hypothesis that abnormal returns are zero, but they differ in the necessary assumptions about the statistical properties of (abnormal) returns. In what follows, we discuss and implement some frequently used tests.[1]

Patell (1976) proposes a test statistic where the event period abnormal returns are standardized by the standard deviation of the estimation period abnormal returns. This standardization reduces the effect of stocks with large return standard deviations on the test. Patell's (1976) test statistic assumes cross-sectional independence in abnormal returns, and it also assumes that there is no event-induced change in the variance of the event-period abnormal returns. The test statistic is calculated as follows:

$$t_{Patell} = \frac{\sum_{i=1}^{N} SR_i}{\sqrt{\sum_{i=1}^{N} \frac{D_i - 2}{D_i - 4}}} \qquad (6.1a)$$

where N is the number of stocks in the portfolio; D_i is the number of observations in stock i's estimation period; and SR_i is the standardized abnormal returns of the ith stock, calculated by dividing the event-period abnormal return on the ith stock on day t by the standard deviation of the estimation-period abnormal returns. The denominator in equation (6.1a) is approximately equal to the square root of the number of firms in the portfolio, which is usually used in actual calculations. In this case, equation (6.1a) can be simplified as follows:

$$t_{Patell} = \frac{\sum_{i=1}^{N} SR_i}{\sqrt{N}} \qquad (6.1b)$$

The ordinary cross-sectional test assumes that there is no cross-sectional dependence in abnormal returns, but allows for event-induced variance changes. The ordinary cross-sectional test is calculated by dividing the mean abnormal return during the event period by its contemporaneous cross-sectional standard error, as in the example presented in Chapter 5.

---

[1] See, for example, Pamela P. Peterson, "Event Studies: A Review of Issues and Methodology," *Quarterly Journal of Business and Economics* 8 (1989): 36-66, and Glenn V. Henderson, Jr., "Problems and Solutions in Conducting Event Studies," *Journal of Risk and Insurance* 57 (1990): 282-306, for reviews of basic event-study methodology.

$$t_{cs} = \frac{\dfrac{1}{N}\sum\limits_{i=1}^{N} AR_i}{\sqrt{\dfrac{1}{N(N-1)}\sum\limits_{i=1}^{N}\left[AR_i - \dfrac{1}{N}\sum\limits_{i=1}^{N} AR_i\right]^2}}$$

(6.2)

where AR_i is the abnormal returns of the ith stock.

The "standardized cross-sectional test" developed by Boehmer et al. (1991) incorporates the information from both the estimation and the event period. The event-period abnormal returns are first standardized by the estimation-period standard deviation as in Patell's test statistic. The cross-sectional technique is then applied to the standardized abnormal returns. Thus, the test statistic takes the following form:

$$t_{BMP} = \frac{\dfrac{1}{N}\sum\limits_{i=1}^{N} SR_i}{\sqrt{\dfrac{1}{N(N-1)}\sum\limits_{i=1}^{N}\left[SR_i - \dfrac{1}{N}\sum\limits_{i=1}^{N} SR_i\right]^2}}$$

(6.3)

where SR_i is the standardized abnormal returns of the ith stock, calculated by dividing the event-period abnormal return on the ith stock on day t by the standard deviation of the estimation-period abnormal returns. Boehmer et al. (1991) show that this test statistic is not affected by event-induced variance changes.

All of these tests are parametric and therefore based on the specific assumptions about the distribution of abnormal returns. Nonparametric tests do not make such assumptions and may be better suited for some analyses. The sign test is a frequently used nonparametric test that is based on the sign of the abnormal return. It assumes that abnormal returns are not cross-correlated and tests the hypothesis that half of abnormal returns are negative. The statistic for the one-sided sign test is

$$t_{sign} = \frac{(P-0.5)}{\sqrt{\dfrac{0.25}{N}}}$$

(6.4)

where P is the proportion of stocks with a positive abnormal return.

The Data

In this chapter we use the same data as in the previous chapter; see the section in Chapter 5 titled "The Data" for details.

Sample Program

Conducting event studies requires many repetitive calculations. Abnormal returns, cumulative abnormal returns, and test statistics are calculated for each firm, each event period, and each day in the event period. Instead of repeating the same programming statements over and over for each firm in the sample, a macro can be used to generate the repeated program statements. The routine for calculating descriptive and test statistics must be written only once. To apply the code to different firms and event windows, the macro is then called repeatedly. This approach makes the program much easier to write and much simpler to follow. The basic programming logic for the event study program is as follows:

- Read the data from an external text file.

- Use the macro ESTUDY to estimate the market model, compute abnormal returns, and compute the associated test statistics.

- Use the macro EVNTRUN, which invokes ESTUDY repeatedly, to compute estimates for various event windows.

Reading and Organizing the Data

The first DATA step reads the sample data into a SAS data set (see the section in Chapter 5 titled "The Data" for a description of the data, and see Chapter 4 for our introduction to SAS macros). Then, as in Chapter 5, we generate a variable that contains the return date measured relative to the event date.

Code 6.1: Read returns data and count pre-event returns

```
* read data from text file;
data returns;
    infile 'c:\edata.dat';
    input firm $ @10 date yymmdd6. @17 evntdate yymmdd6. evntdum $ ret
    mrktret;
    format date evntdate yymmdd6.;
    before = date < evntdate;
    if evntdum = '1' then evntdum = 'neg';
    if evntdum = '2' then evntdum = 'pos';

* sort and determine number of days with data before event date;
proc sort data=returns;
    by firm evntdate date;
proc means data=returns noprint;
    by firm evntdate;
    output out=nreturns (drop=_type_ _freq_) sum(before)= bef_sum;
```

The new data set RETURNS contains the following variables:

FIRM	Firm-specific CUSIP
DATE	Return date
EVNTDATE	Event date
EVNTDUM	A portfolio code that indicates whether the announced earnings were below/above the expected earnings
RET	Daily stock return
MRKRET	Daily market return
BEFORE	This dummy variable has a one for all days before the event

The PROC MEANS step, as in Chapter 5, creates a new data set NRETURNS that contains firm-event identifiers and the variable BEF_SUM, which contains the number of pre-event return days. This is important, because in practice some firms often have fewer return days available than others. For the program to work appropriately, it is still required that the return series for each firm consist of contiguous entries for each trading day (which of course may include missing values).

Next, we define the beginning of the main macro that executes the event study and split the data into estimation-period and event-period records.

Code 6.2: Macro ESTUDY—definition

```
%macro estudy(ds=,subgroup=);
%let evntdays = %eval(&end-&start+1);
```

The %MACRO ESTUDY(DS=,SUBGROUP=) statement defines the macro ESTUDY and two macro variables. Here, the variables represent the return data set and an indicator variable. In our example, it classifies firms as positive and negative earnings surprises. Values for the macro variables are assigned when the macro is invoked. We will assign the value RETURN to the variable DS, because this data set contains our returns. Similarly, we will assign the value EVNTDUM to the variable SUBGROUP, because it contains the dummy variable indicating the sign of the unexpected earnings.

The first macro statement defines the variable EVNTDAYS, which represents the number of days in the event period. The %LET statement computes a value for EVNTDAYS, based on the beginning and ending day of the event period. The beginning and ending days are expressed as days relative to the event day and stored in the macro variables START and END. Both are defined later in the program. For example, to analyze abnormal returns from day −2 to day +1 relative to the announcement day, the value of EVNTDAYS is determined as follows:

```
%LET evntdays = %eval(&end–&start+1)
    = 1 – (–2) + 1
    = 4
```

Next, we create different data sets for the estimation and event periods.

Code 6.3: Macro ESTUDY—Divide data into estimation and event periods

```
* compute event date counter and split data into estimation and event
periods;
data estper evntper;
    merge &ds (drop=before) n&ds;
    by firm evntdate;
    if first.evntdate then relday=-bef_sum - 1;
    relday + 1;
    if relday < -10 then output estper;
    if &start <= relday <= &end then output evntper;
```

As in the previous chapter, the MERGE statement merges each observation in RETURNS, which has several records per event, with each observation in NRETURNS, which has one record per event. As a result, the matching records from the latter are repeated for each daily return record. We use the BY statement in the DATA step to make the automatic variables available that indicate the beginning and end of each BY group. Here, whenever the first record for an event is read, the new variable RELDAY is set to the number of pre-event days (minus one, and the next line adds one again). This variable now contains the relative days we need to subset the estimation and event periods: ESTPER contains estimation period data (more than 10 trading days before the event), and EVNTPER contains the returns for the period later defined by the macro variables START and END.

Estimating the Market Model Parameters

The next section of the program estimates the market model coefficients that are needed to calculate abnormal returns.

Code 6.4: Macro ESTUDY—Estimate market model parameters

```
* compute market model parameters in estimation period;
proc reg data=estper outest=mmparam (rename=(intercept=alpha mrktret=beta)
    keep=firm evntdate intercept mrktret _rmse_) noprint;
    by firm evntdate;
    model ret = mrktret;
quit;
```

PROC REG estimates the market model parameters and writes the results to the new data set MMPARAM. The BY statement results in separate regressions for each earnings announcement, and the MODEL statement defines the regression of daily stock returns on daily market returns. The estimates for coefficients and root mean square error are written to the output data set, and the default variables names are changed for the coefficient estimates using the RENAME data set option. MMPARAM now contains one set of market model estimates per firm-event combination.

The next step is to first compute and then cumulate abnormal returns during the event period.

Code 6.5: Macro ESTUDY—Calculate abnormal returns

```
* compute abnormal returns in event period;
data ar;
     merge evntper mmparam;
     by firm evntdate;
     ar  = ret - alpha - beta * mrktret;
     estpvar = _rmse_ * _rmse_;

* compute cumulative abnormal returns;
proc means data=ar noprint;
     by firm evntdate;
     id &subgroup estpvar;
     output out=car sum(ar)=car;

* define additional variables for hypothesis tests;
data car1;
     set car;
     cardummy = car>0;
     scar     = car / (sqrt(&evntdays * estpvar));
```

The MERGE statement combines the data set EVNTPER (the daily stock returns for the event period) with MMPARAM (the estimated market model parameters). The BY statement merges each daily return record with the corresponding set of market model estimates. This is an example of one-to-many merging: each event has only one market model record, but several return records. The MERGE-BY statements "fill up" each return observation with the corresponding market model estimates by duplicating the latter as often as necessary.

Next, abnormal returns, AR, are computed based on event-period returns and the estimated coefficients from the estimation period. For each event, PROC MEANS sums abnormal returns over the event period and writes the results to the new data set CAR. The BY statement lets PROC MEANS produce one output record for each event and each subgroup. Note that we use the ID statement to add two important variables to the output data set: the estimation-period variance, ESTPVAR, and the grouping variable defined by SUBGROUP. By default, PROC MEANS includes only the analysis variables (and BY variables, if present) in the output data set.

The subsequent DATA step uses this output data set and adds two variables that are necessary to compute some of the test statistics. The first one, CARDUMMY, is a simple indicator (dummy) variable for positive returns. It will be used to calculate the sign test statistics. The second new variable, SCAR, contains standardized abnormal returns (or standardized cumulative abnormal returns), *SR*, used in Patell's (1976) and Boehmer et al.'s (1991) test statistics (see equations 6.1a, 6.1b, and 6.3). The variance of the estimation-period abnormal return (ESTPVAR) is multiplied by the number of days in the event period (EVNTDAYS). Then the abnormal return is divided by the square root of this product.

Calculating Portfolio Abnormal Returns and Test Statistics

The next step is to compute test statistics and abnormal returns for the portfolios of positive and negative unexpected earnings.

Code 6.6: Macro ESTUDY—Calculate test statistics and abnormal returns for portfolios

```
* if the analysis contrasts two groups, sort by group now;
%if "&subgroup" ne "" %then %do;
proc sort data=car1;
    by &subgroup;
%end;


* compute statistics by group - if none is requested, BY statement is
ignored;
proc means data=car1 noprint;
    by &subgroup ;
    var car scar cardummy;
    output out=test
mean (car scar cardummy) = mcar mscar percpos
n    (car scar cardummy) = ncar nscar npercpos
t    (car scar)          = tcs  tbmp;
```

We are analyzing the event-period abnormal returns from the data set CAR1. Note that the variable CAR refers either to the daily abnormal return or to the cumulative abnormal return. This depends on how the variables START and END are defined when invoking the macro ESTUDY (discussed below). First, the data must be sorted by the grouping variable so we can use it in BY statements. Note that PROC SORT is executed only if a grouping variable is actually passed to the macro—if abnormal returns for the entire sample are computed, this sorting is not necessary.

Next, PROC MEANS is used to compute means, the number of observations, and *t*-statistics for the variables CAR, SCAR, and CARDUMMY. The OUTPUT statement requests that the results be written to the data set TEST. Using the OUTPUT keywords, we compute the following new variables:

mcar   The average (cumulative) abnormal return of the stocks in a
portfolio. Our null hypothesis is that firms with positive
unexpected earnings should have positive abnormal returns, and
firms with negative unexpected earnings should have negative
abnormal returns.

mscar   The average standarized abnormal return. This variable is
needed when calculating Patell's (1976) test statistic (see
variable *SR* in equations 6.1a and 6.1b).

percpos   The proportion of positive abnormal returns in a
portfolio. This variable will be needed when calculating the
sign test statistics.

ncar, nscar, These variables indicate the number of firms in a portfolio.
npercpos   If there are no missing observations for any of the variables
in the VAR statement, the values of the variables are equal.

tcs   The cross-sectional test statistic as described in equation (6.2). It
is calculated from a cross section of event-period abnormal returns.

tbmp   The standardized cross-sectional test statistic developed by Boehmer
et al. (1991), as described in equation (6.3). It corresponds to
the *t*-statistic calculated from a cross section of event-period
standardized abnormal returns.

Calculating and Printing the Main Results

We have now computed most of the necessary variables, but some additional calculations
need to be performed to obtain the final statistics. The next DATA step does that and also
labels the resulting variables. While not shown in our example, this step can also be used to
compute additional statistics or, for example, significance levels. SAS offers functions that
compute the fractiles for most distributions. These functions can be used to define new
variables, corresponding to each test statistic, that contain their significance levels.

Code 6.7: Macro ESTUDY—Print abnormal returns and associated test statistics

```
* arrange output data set and compute more test statistics, then print;
data results;
    set test;
    tpatell = mscar * sqrt(nscar);
    tsign   = (percpos-0.5) / sqrt(0.25/npercpos);
    label tpatell = 'patell´s (1976) t-statistic';
    label mcar    = 'average abnormal return';
    label tcs     = 'cross-sectional t-statistic';
    label tbmp    = 'boehmer´s et al. (1991) t-statistic';
    label ncar    = 'number of events in the portfolio';
    label percpos = 'percent positive abnormal return';
    label tsign   = 'sign-test statistic';

proc print label u;
    id &subgroup;
    title1 "output for data set &ds for a (&start,&end) window";
    var mcar ncar percpos tsign tpatell tcs tbmp;
```

Patell's (1976) test statistic (equation 6.1b) is assigned to the variable TPATELL. The test statistic is equal to the average standardized abnormal return multiplied by the square root of the number of events in the portfolio. The sign test (equation 6.4) is assigned to the variable TSIGN. The LABEL statements define the names of the variables for the printed output.

Finally, PROC PRINT is used to display the results of the event study in the SAS output. The LABEL option requests that variable labels, and not their names, be used as column headings in the output. The UNIFORM option requests uniform formatting for each output page. The ID statement uses the values of the SUBGROUP variable to identify observations in the output. Note the use of macro variables DS, START and END in the TITLE1 statement. They are used inside the title text string so that titles display information about the specific values of the macro variables used. The VAR statement defines which variables should be printed and also determines their order in the output.

The event study macro is now essentially complete. To illustrate its accomplishments, we present its output for an analysis of only the event day (day 0). We discuss next how tests across groups are performed, and then, finally, how the macro is invoked.

Output 6.1: Results of analyzing the average abnormal returns of the two portfolios on the earnings announcement day

```
              Output for data set returns for a (0,0) window
              Analysis for portfolios according to evntdum

                                Number of     Percent
                     Average    events in     positive
                     abnormal      the         abnormal    Sign-test
         evntdum     return     portfolio      return      statistic
           NEG      -.001074367     148         0.51351      0.32880
           POS      0.003044564     176         0.58523      2.26134


                     Patell's                            Boehmer's et
                      (1976)     Cross-sectional          al. (1991)
         evntdum    t-statistic    t-statistic           t-statistic
           NEG       -0.56054       -0.51608               -0.33122
           POS        2.68897        1.70938                1.81984
```

The table shows two rows of estimates: the first (NEG) is for the portfolio of negative earnings surprises, the second (POS) for positive surprises. The average abnormal return for the former is −0.107% and 0.304% for the latter. The column "Number of events in portfolio" reports the number of observations in both of the portfolios. There are 148 earnings announcements in the portfolio of negative unexpected earnings, and 176 earnings announcements in the portfolio of positive unexpected earnings. The column "Percent positive abnormal returns" reports the fraction of announcements with positive abnormal returns. We find that 51.35% of negative surprises and 58.52% of positive surprises generate positive abnormal returns on day 0.

Two of the test statistics are significant for positive surprises, and none is significant for negative surprises. Among the former, there is some disagreement among the test statistics: the sign test and Patell's test are significant at the 5% level, but the other two statistics are not. Thus, we find no evidence of negative reactions after negative surprises, and some evidence that a positive reaction is associated with positive surprises.

Comparing Portfolio Abnormal Returns

In most event studies it makes sense to statistically compare the returns of different groups/portfolios. Specifically, we would like to test whether the abnormal returns of the portfolios are significantly different from each other.

Code 6.8: Macro ESTUDY—Test the difference of abnormal returns across portfolios and end the macro definition

```
* if groups are contrasted, test for equality across groups;
%if "&subgroup" ne "" %then %do;
    title2 "analysis for portfolios according to &subgroup";

proc ttest data=car1;
    var scar;
    class &subgroup;
proc npar1way data=car1 wilcoxon;
    var scar;
    class &subgroup;
%end;


run;
%mend estudy;
```

Note that the statements above are executed only if a grouping variable is passed to the macro when it is invoked. If no grouping variable is present (i.e., SUBGROUP is missing), no statements are executed. PROC TTEST performs a two-sample *t*-test to test the null hypothesis that mean returns are equal across two portfolios. PROC NPAR1WAY performs a variety of nonparametric tests, even across multiple portfolios. In this example, we use PROC NPAR1WAY to compute a Wilcoxon rank-sum test.

The last statement, %MEND, marks the end of the macro definition. We have now discussed the program necessary to generate some event study results.

Invoking the Main Macro

Since we have completed the macro ESTUDY, all that remains to be done is to write a routine to invoke ESTUDY in a way that makes it easy to analyze different event windows. Recall that we started the macro definition with the statement %MACRO ESTUDY (DS=,SUBGROUP=). When the macro is invoked, we can pass values to the macro variables DS and SUBGROUP. We also must assign values to the variables START and END that define the first and last day of the event period. Because in most cases it is instructive to analyze event windows of varying lengths, the macro ESTUDY must be invoked several times with different values for the START and END variables. To do that, we use a second macro EVNTRUN.

Code 6.9: Define event windows to analyze and invoke the event-study macro

```
* define event windows that the macro should analyze;

%macro evntrun(dataset=,portf=);
* first compute daily one-day statistics;
%do i = 0 %to 0;
    %let start = &i;
    %let end   = &i;
    %estudy(ds=&dataset,subgroup=&portf)
%end;

* then compute multi-day cumulative statistics;
%let start = -3;
%let end   =  1;
%estudy(ds=&dataset,subgroup=&portf)
%mend evntrun;

* start the program;
%evntrun(dataset=returns,portf=evntdum)
```

The iterative %DO loop is used to invoke the macro ESTUDY several times with different values of variables %START and %LET. Each time the iterative %DO loop executes, the macro processor assigns the value of I to both START and END. Because the value of I in the example ranges only from 0 to 0, the loop executes once and performs all estimations in ESTUDY (these one-day results are not shown). The next group of statements defines a longer event window ranging from day −3 to day +1. These results are reported in Output 6.2. Finally, the %MEND statement ends the macro definition, and %EVNTRUN(DATASET=RETURNS,PORTF=EVNTDUM) invokes it and passes on the name of the data set and the name of the portfolio indicator.

Output 6.2: Cumulative abnormal returns and test statistics for positive and negative earnings surprises over the window (–3 to +1)

```
                  Output for data set returns for a (-3,1) window
                  Analysis for portfolios according to evntdum


                                Number of     Percent
                                events in     positive
                      Average       the       abnormal     Sign-test
           evntdum    abnormal    portfolio     return     statistic
                       return
             NEG     -.004854029     148        0.50676     0.16440
             POS     0.007996778     176        0.55682     1.50756


                        Patell's                        Boehmer et
                         (1976)      Cross-sectional    al.'s (1991)
           evntdum     t-statistic     t-statistic      t-statistic
             NEG       -1.42504         -1.07926          -0.89150
             POS        3.45707          2.43076           2.71423


                  Output for data set returns for a (-3,1) window
                  Analysis for portfolios according to evntdum

                            The TTEST Procedure
                                Statistics


                                Lower CL            Upper CL  Lower CL
  Variable  evntdum       N       Mean     Mean       Mean    Std Dev   Std Dev
  SCAR      NEG          148     -0.377   -0.117     0.1425    1.4348    1.5985
  SCAR      POS          176      0.0711   0.2606    0.4501    1.1531    1.2737
  SCAR      Diff (1-2)           -0.692   -0.378    -0.064     1.3286    1.4311


                                Upper CL
           Variable  evntdum    Std Dev    Std Err   Minimum    Maximum
           SCAR      NEG         1.8047     0.1314    -5.89      4.3682
           SCAR      POS         1.4227     0.096     -2.773     4.4023
           SCAR      Diff (1-2)  1.5509     0.1596


                                 T-Tests


           Variable   Method        Variances    DF   t Value   Pr > |t|
           SCAR       Pooled        Equal        322   -2.37     0.0185
           SCAR       Satterthwaite Unequal      279   -2.32     0.0210
```

Output 6.2 (continued)

```
                        Equality of Variances

        Variable    Method      Num DF    Den DF    F Value    Pr > F
        SCAR        Folded F       147       175       1.58    0.0040




             Output for data set returns for a (-3,1) window
             Analysis for portfolios according to evntdum

                       The NPAR1WAY Procedure

            Wilcoxon Scores (Rank Sums) for Variable SCAR
                  Classified by Variable evntdum


                        Sum of      Expected      Std Dev        Mean
        evntdum    N    Scores      Under H0      Under H0       Score
        NEG      148   22543.0       24050.0    839.920631  152.317568
        POS      176   30107.0       28600.0    839.920631  171.062500


                   Wilcoxon Two-Sample Test

              Statistic               22543.0000

              Normal Approximation
              Z                          -1.7936
              One-Sided Pr <  Z           0.0364
              Two-Sided Pr > |Z|          0.0729

              t Approximation
              One-Sided Pr <  Z           0.0369
              Two-Sided Pr > |Z|          0.0738

          Z includes a continuity correction of 0.5.

                   Kruskal-Wallis Test

              Chi-Square                  3.2192
              DF                               1
              Pr > Chi-Square             0.0728
```

We obtain similar results for the four-day window as for the event day alone. The parametric tests imply that positive earnings surprises are associated with significantly positive abnormal returns; negative surprises do not cause abnormal performance.

The second part of the output shows the results of PROC TTEST. Following the descriptive statistics, it shows that the mean SCAR is significantly larger for positive surprises. Equality of variances across groups is rejected, but this has little effect on the means test: under both assumptions (equal/unequal variance), the means test is significant.

Finally, the third part of the output is generated by PROC NPAR1WAY. It first lists the rank sums (Wilcoxon scores). As we would expect from the previous analysis, positive surprises have higher than expected scores, and vice versa for negative surprises. The difference across groups, however, is only marginally significant at 7.38% for the two-sided test.

Program Listing

```
* read data from text file;
data returns;
    infile 'c:\edata.dat';
    input firm $ @10 date yymmdd6. @17 evntdate yymmdd6. evntdum $ ret
mrktret;
    format date evntdate yymmdd6.;
    before = date < evntdate;
    if evntdum = '1' then evntdum = 'neg';
    if evntdum = '2' then evntdum = 'pos';

* sort and determine number of days with data before event date;
proc sort data=returns;
    by firm evntdate date;
proc means data=returns noprint;
    by firm evntdate;
    output out=nreturns (drop=_type_ _freq_) sum(before)= bef_sum;

%macro estudy(ds=,subgroup=);
%let evntdays = %eval(&end-&start+1);

* compute event date counter and split data into estimation and event
periods;
data estper evntper;
    merge &ds (drop=before) n&ds;
    by firm evntdate;
    if first.evntdate then relday=-bef_sum - 1;
    relday + 1;
    if relday < -10 then output estper;
    if &start <= relday <= &end then output evntper;

* compute market model parameters in estimation period;
proc reg data=estper outest=mmparam (rename=(intercept=alpha mrktret=beta)
    keep=firm evntdate intercept mrktret _rmse_) noprint;
    by firm evntdate;
```

```
       model ret = mrktret;
quit;

* compute abnormal returns in event period;
data ar;
     merge evntper mmparam;
     by firm evntdate;
     ar  = ret - alpha - beta * mrktret;
     estpvar = _rmse_ * _rmse_;

* compute cumulative abnormal returns;
proc means data=ar noprint;
     by firm evntdate;
     id &subgroup estpvar;
     output out=car sum(ar)=car;

* define additional variables for hypothesis tests;
data car1;
     set car;
     cardummy = car>0;
     scar     = car / (sqrt(&evntdays * estpvar));

* if the analysis contrasts two groups, sort by group now;
%if "&subgroup" ne "" %then %do;
proc sort data=car1;
     by &subgroup;
%end;

* compute statistics by group - if none is requested, BY statement is
ignored;
proc means data=car1 noprint;
     by &subgroup ;
     var car scar cardummy;
     output out=test
mean (car scar cardummy) = mcar mscar percpos
n    (car scar cardummy) = ncar nscar npercpos
t    (car scar)          = tcs  tbmp;

* arrange output data set and compute more test statistics, then print;
data results;
     set test;
     tpatell = mscar * sqrt(nscar);
     tsign   = (percpos-0.5) / sqrt(0.25/npercpos);
     label tpatell = 'patell´s (1976) t-statistic';
     label mcar    = 'average abnormal return';
     label tcs     = 'cross-sectional t-statistic';
     label tbmp    = 'boehmer´s et al. (1991) t-statistic';
     label ncar    = 'number of events in the portfolio';
     label percpos = 'percent positive abnormal return';
     label tsign   = 'sign-test statistic';
```

```
proc print label u;
    id &subgroup;
    title1 "output for data set &ds for a (&start,&end) window";
    var mcar ncar percpos tsign tpatell tcs tbmp;

* if groups are contrasted, test for equality across groups;
%if "&subgroup" ne "" %then %do;
    title2 "analysis for portfolios according to &subgroup";

proc ttest data=car1;
    var scar;
    class &subgroup;
proc npar1way data=car1 wilcoxon;
    var scar;
    class &subgroup;
%end;


run;
%mend estudy;

* define event windows that the macro should analyze;

%macro evntrun(dataset=,portf=);
* first compute daily one-day statistics;
%do i = 0 %to 0;
    %let start = &i;
    %let end   = &i;
    %estudy(ds=&dataset,subgroup=&portf)
%end;


* then compute multi-day cumulative statistics;
%let start = -3;
%let end   = 1;
%estudy(ds=&dataset,subgroup=&portf)
%mend evntrun;

* start the program;
%evntrun(dataset=returns,portf=evntdum)
```

CHAPTER 7

ASSOCIATION TYPES OF STUDIES: INVESTIGATING THE PRICE-EARNINGS RELATIONSHIP

> **Key Concepts**
> - Earnings response coefficients
> - Cross-sectional and time-series regressions
>
> **Data Concepts**
> - Monthly stock returns and prices
> - Annual earnings

Background for Association Types of Studies

The relationship between stock prices or returns and accounting earnings is usually investigated through association or event study approaches (see, for instance, Collins and Kothari 1989). In association types of studies, returns measured over long time periods (e.g., fiscal years) are regressed on unexpected earnings. A short-term stock market response to the earnings announcement is investigated by using the event study approach discussed in the previous chapters. Some studies also use the price-earnings regression approach to investigate short-term market responses. The following regression model illustrates the concept of the investigation of the price-earnings relationship:

$$AR_{it} = \alpha + \beta UX_{it} + e_{it} \tag{7.1}$$

where AR_{it} is the abnormal return on the *i*th firm for period *t*; UX_{it} denotes the unexpected earnings of the *i*th firm for period *t*; α is an intercept term; β is the estimated slope coefficient, also referred to as the earnings response coefficient (ERC); and e_{it} is an error term with zero mean and constant variance. Several alternative specifications of the basic price-earnings regression model are suggested in the literature. The main alternatives can roughly be classified into two categories: price models, where stock prices are regressed on earnings-per-share figures; and return models, where stock returns are regressed on scaled earnings.

Studies estimating the price-earnings regressions are interested in the significance of the estimated ERC and the explanatory power of the model. The estimated ERC should be statistically significantly different from zero, if accounting earnings are related to stock returns. From an economic point of view, the estimated ERC should be the reciprocal of the firm's expected rate of return. Therefore, some studies compare the estimated ERCs to the firm's expected rate of return estimated in different ways.

The typical research design for this type of study regresses annual stock returns (or end-of-the-year prices) on the contemporaneous year's earnings. Some studies also use returns from the previous period in the regressions, because it has been observed that stock prices lead accounting earnings. Next we briefly review some of the model specifications used in selected classical studies in the area.

Kothari and Zimmerman (1995) compared the so-called price and return models. In price models, stock prices are regressed on earnings-per-share (eps) figures, whereas in return models, stock returns are regressed on scaled earnings. They use the following model specifications:

$$P_t = \alpha^a + \beta^a X_t + e_t^a \qquad (7.2a)$$

$$P_t / P_{t-1} = \alpha^b + \beta^b X_t / P_{t-1} + e_t^b \qquad (7.2b)$$

$$\Delta P_t = \alpha^c + \beta^c \Delta X_t + e_t^c \qquad (7.2c)$$

where P_t is the stock price at the end of year *t*, X_t is the annual earnings per share in year *t*, P_{t-1} is the stock price at the end of year *t*–1, ΔX_t is the change in annual earnings in year *t*, α is an intercept term, β is the estimated slope coefficient (the earnings response coefficient), and e_t is an error term. Note that the price relative, P_t / P_{t-1}, equals one plus the annual return over the fiscal year.

Model (7.2a) is a price model, because it has a stock price as a dependent variable. In the same way, model (7.2b) is a return model, because stock return (price relative) is used as a dependent variable. Model (7.2c) is the differenced-price model.

Kothari and Zimmerman (1995) find that the ERCs are substantially less biased in price models than in returns models. However, heteroscedasticity and model misspecifications cause more problems for price models than for return models. So researchers should consider using both price models and returns models to ensure that the empirical results are not sensitive to the way the model is specified.

Kothari (1992) investigates the alternative returns-earnings regression specifications under the assumption that stock prices lead accounting earnings—that is, stock prices reflect information about future earnings that are not involved in past earnings. The main models he uses are as follows (we use primes to differentiate the coefficients from those in equations 7.2a–7.2c):

$$P_t / P_{t-1} = \alpha'^a + \beta'^a X_t / P_{t-1} + e'^a_t \tag{7.3a}$$

$$P_t / P_{t-1} = \alpha'^b + \beta'^b \Delta X_t / P_{t-1} + e'^b_t \tag{7.3b}$$

$$P_t / P_{t-1} = \alpha'^c + \beta'^c \Delta X_t / X_{t-1} + e'^c_t \tag{7.3c}$$

where P_t is the stock price at the end of year t, P_{t-1} is the stock price at the end of year $t-1$, X_t is the annual earnings per share in year t, X_{t-1} is the annual earnings per share in year $t-1$, ΔX_{it} is the change in annual earnings in year t, α' is an intercept term, β' is the earnings response coefficient, and e'_t is an error term. Note that model (7.3a) is equal to model (7.2b).

Kothari (1992) reports that the inclusion of leading-period returns in the price-earnings regressions reduces estimation bias in the estimated ERCs. As a result ERCs increase as leading-period returns are included in the price-earnings regressions. He also finds that longer return measurement intervals yield less biased estimates of the ERCs.

The Data

The sample data are retrieved from Compustat and CRSP for the period 1979 to 1998. The firms are those included in the S&P 500 Index. Annual earnings (excluding extraordinary items and earnings from discontinued operations) per share are from Compustat. Monthly stock prices are from the CRSP. Both earnings and stock prices are corrected for stock splits and other distributions.

Sample SAS Code for Price-Earnings Regressions

Reading the Data

Our sample SAS program can be used to estimate both price models and return models. The code includes examples of cross-sectional, time-series, and pooled (panel) estimation of the models. Our goal is to illustrate how SAS can be used in this type of research. An in-depth econometric analysis and discussion of the estimation of alternative model specifications are beyond the scope of this book.

The sample program begins with a routine for reading the stock market and accounting data from text files. We also define some variables that are needed when combining the data sets.

Code 7.1: Read the financial statement data and return data

```
* read compustat data from text file;
data cs;
     infile 'c:\comperc.dat';
     input firm $ year eps1 adjfac;
     eps = eps1/adjfac;
     drop eps1 adjfac;

* read crsp data from text file and keep only year-end returns;
data crsp;
     infile 'c:\crsperc.dat';
     input firm $ date yymmdd8. return price mv;
     format date yymmdd6.;
     price = abs(price);
     year = year(date);
     month = month(date);
     if month = 12;
     drop return mv;
```

The two DATA steps read the Compustat and CRSP data from text files into two new data sets. The first data set, CS, contains earnings per share; the second data set, CRSP, contains stock prices. Both data sets include additional variables that uniquely identify firms and time periods. We again use SAS date formats to read in the stock-price dates from the text file, where they are stored as *yyyymmdd*. Then we apply the functions YEAR and MONTH to extract the year and month, respectively. The new variables YEAR and MONTH are numeric variables of the form *yyyy* and *mm*, respectively. Next, we use the latter variable to select only end-of-year stock prices: because we need only annual returns, the subsetting IF statement in the second DATA step selects only December (i.e., end-of-year) records. We use the following variables:

```
FIRM  Firm identifier (CUSIP)
YEAR  Year (YYYY)
EPS   Earnings per share
DATE  Stock-price date (YYYYMMDD)
PRICE End-of-month stock price
```

Defining Variables for Price-Earnings Regressions

Next, we need to combine the two data sets. They are first sorted by firm and year and then merged. The new combined data set ALLDATA contains both the stock market and the accounting information we need for the price-earnings regressions. We also define additional variables for the regressions.

Code 7.2: Define variables for earnings regressions

```
* combine compustat and crsp data;
proc sort data=cs;
    by firm year;
proc sort data=crsp;
    by firm date;
data alldata;
    merge cs crsp;
    by firm year;
    lagprice = lag (price);
    lageps   = lag (eps);
    difprice = dif (price);
    difeps   = dif (eps);
    if eps =. or price =. then delete;
    if first.firm then do;
    lagprice =.; lageps =.; difprice =.; difeps =.;
end;
    anret    = price  / lagprice;
    defleps  = eps    / lagprice;
    defldif  = difeps / lagprice;
    deflchng = difeps / abs(lageps);
```

The data set ALLDATA is created by combining the data set CS, which contains the earnings figures, and the data set CRSP, which contains stock prices. The conditional DELETE statement removes all observations with missing values of earnings or stock prices. Lagged stock prices and earnings-per-share figures are created with the LAG function. For instance, if the previous year's eps for a certain firm is equal to 4.5, the variable LAGEPS gets this value in the current year. Similarly, the DIF function creates first differences.

Note that we lose the first observation of the time series when using the lagged or difference variables. The way we assign the values to the variables LAGPRICE, LAGEPS, DIFPRICE, and DIFEPS does not take this into account. For a given firm, the first observation of the lagged and difference variables gets their values from the last observation of the previous firm! Because we do not intend to mix observations from different firms, we reset the lagged variables to missing whenever we encounter the first record of a new firm.

The program then defines the following variables for the regressions:

ANRET	One plus the annual (year-end) return. This is the dependent variable in models (7.2b), (7.3a), (7.3b), and (7.3c).
DEFLEPS	Earnings per share in year t deflated by the stock price at the end of year $t-1$. This is the independent variable in models (7.2b) and (7.3a).
DEFLDIF	Change in earnings per share between two successive years deflated by stock price at the end of year $t-1$. This is the independent variable in model (7.3b).
DEFLCHNG	Percentage change in earnings from year $t-1$ to year t. The ABS function takes the absolute value of the lagged earnings figure to avoid the problems associated with negative deflators. The variable DEFLCHNG is the independent variable in model (7.3c).

Deleting Extreme Observations and Printing Summary Statistics

The program continues with a routine for deleting extreme observations of all variables and printing descriptive statistics for each variable. We exclude observations with values smaller than the 1st percentile or larger than the 99th percentile. This cutoff point is of course arbitrary, but it is frequently used in related studies. Empirical economists disagree widely on whether winsorization is appropriate; we do employ it here to illustrate how winsorization can be implemented in SAS. It is straightforward to modify the program to use other cutoff points and winsorize each year or each firm. Empirically, the results we report below are qualitatively unchanged by winsorization, but it almost doubles the adjusted R^2 of several regressions.

Code 7.3: Winsorization and descriptive statistics

```
* winsorize earnings and prices, then merge percentiles with data;
proc means noprint data=alldata;
    var price eps difprice difeps anret defleps defldif deflchng;
    output out=extremes (drop=_type_ _freq_)
    p1  = lprice leps ldifpri ldifeps lanret ldefleps ldefldif ldeflchn
    p99 = hprice heps hdifpri hdifeps hanret hdefleps hdefldif hdeflchn;

data windata;
    if _n_=1 then set extremes;
    set alldata;
    if price > hprice or price < lprice then delete;
    if eps > heps or eps < leps then delete;
    if difprice > hdifpri or difprice < ldifpri then delete;
    if difeps > hdifeps or difeps < ldifeps then delete;
    if anret > hanret or anret < lanret then delete;
    if defleps > hdefleps or defleps < ldefleps then delete;
    if defldif > hdefldif or defldif < ldefldif then delete;
    if deflchng > hdeflchn or deflchng < ldeflchn then delete;
```

Code 7.3 (continued)

```
proc sort data=windata;
    by year;

* descriptive statistics;
proc means n min mean max std data=windata;
    title "descriptive statistics for winsorized data";
    var price eps difprice difeps anret defleps defldif deflchng;
```

PROC MEANS is used to determine the 1st and 99th percentiles for each variable. The OUTPUT statement creates a new data set EXTREMES that contains the cutoff values for the quantiles of each variable. Keywords P1 and P99 define the names of the variables indicating the extreme one percent quantiles. For instance, variables LPRICE and HPRICE refer to the 1st and 99th price percentiles, respectively. Other keywords (P5, P10, P90, P95...) can be used to change the cutoff points for the empirical analysis.

The data set WINDATA contains the original data and also the percentiles computed in the previous step. Note that EXTREMES has only one observation, and we would like to add this record to each observation in the ALLDATA file. To do that, we use one-to-many merging; in the DATA step, this can be accomplished by using two SET statements. The first one reads the one-observation data set, and the second one reads the longer file. Most importantly, SAS must be instructed to read the one-record file only once when it reads the first observation (i.e., when the automatic variable _N_ equals 1). This causes SAS to fill up the remaining observations of ALLDATA with the single record from EXTREMES (without this condition, the combined data set would have only one observation).

After each record contains both the variable values and their sample percentiles, we exclude all observations where one of the variables has an extreme value. For instance, the IF PRICE > HPRICE OR PRICE < LPRICE THEN DELETE statement excludes all observations with stock prices that are larger (smaller) than the 99th (1st) percentile.

Next, we sort the data by year and produce summary statistics for all variables. Options in the PROC MEANS statement request the following statistics: the number of observations (N), minimum values (MIN), mean values (MEAN), maximum values (MAX), and standard deviation (STD). Results across the 3391 firm-year combinations are shown in Output 7.1.

Output 7.1: Summary statistics of price and earnings variables

```
                    Descriptive statistics for winsorized data
                              The MEANS Procedure

    Variable     N       Minimum        Mean         Maximum       Std Dev
    PRICE      3391     7.1300000     43.1384075    122.2500000    20.4015573
    EPS        3391    -4.2400000      1.2359457      6.4400000     1.2422144
    DIFPRICE   3391   -52.6300000      1.0643232     37.5000000    13.0584944
    DIFEPS     3391    -5.8300000      0.0092923      5.4000000     1.0421302
    ANRET      3391     0.3859649      1.0641723      2.1392949     0.2864843
    DEFLEPS    3391    -0.1756522      0.0309852      0.1833708     0.0333405
    DEFLDIF    3391    -0.1948126    0.000085550      0.2092912     0.0317091
    DEFLCHNG   3391    -6.4761905      0.2792694     19.5357143     1.6109623
```

Estimating Annual Price-Earnings Regressions

Next, we estimate annual cross-sectional price-earnings regressions. This is a frequently applied approach in the literature. Cross-sectional regressions are estimated for each year in the sample period resulting in a time series of estimated annual coefficients. Conclusions and statistical tests are based on their distributions.

We estimate model (7.2a) for each year, save the estimated coefficients to new data sets, and calculate the means of the annual estimates over the years. We only estimate model (7.2a); the program can easily be modified for the other models.

Code 7.4: Annual cross-sectional price-earnings regressions

```
*** annual price and return models ;
* price model (2a);
proc reg outest=model2a  noprint rsquare data=windata;
    model price = eps / spec;
    by year;
proc means n mean t prt min max std data=model2a;
    title "mean coefficients of annual price-earnings regressions";
    var intercept eps _rsq_;
```

PROC REG estimates the price model described in model (7.2a), and the OUTEST option saves the estimated parameters to the data set MODEL2A. The NOPRINT option suppresses the printing of the results of the annual regressions. The RSQUARE options also saves the regression R-squares.

The MODEL PRICE = EPS statement defines the regression equation. Since we are estimating model (7.2a), we regress stock prices (PRICE) on the earnings-per-share figures (EPS). The BY YEAR statement is needed to perform the regressions for each of the years in the sample period. To estimate the other price and return models that we described at the beginning of the chapter, only the MODEL statement would need to be changed accordingly (see the program listing at the end of this chapter).

The data set MODEL2A contains annual estimates of the regression coefficients. We are interested in the estimated intercepts (INTERCEPT), slope coefficients (EPS), and R-squares (_RSQ_). The estimated slope is the earnings response coefficient, ERC, and it is named according to the independent variable EPS.

PROC MEANS is used to compute summary information on the annual estimates. The results for the "price" model (7.2a) are shown in Output 7.2. They indicate that the time-series average of the estimated earnings response coefficient (ERC) is 3.983 with a *t*-value of 9.49, which is significantly different from zero (assuming that the annual estimates are independent and identically distributed). The minimum and maximum annual ERCs are 0.535 and 6.608, respectively. The average R^2 is relatively low (0.065) for a price model.

Output 7.2: Results of annual cross-sectional price-earnings regressions

```
          Mean coefficients of annual price-earnings regressions
                        The MEANS Procedure

Variable    Label         N         Mean   t Value   Pr > |t|       Minimum
Intercept   Intercept    19   37.9725671     57.17     <.0001     33.5224131
EPS                      19    3.9832365      9.49     <.0001      0.5351890
_RSQ_       R-squared    19    0.0651119      5.44     <.0001      0.0010054


            Variable    Label           Maximum        Std Dev
            Intercept   Intercept     43.9785870      2.8949482
            EPS                        6.6079842      1.8296151
            _RSQ_       R-squared      0.1887976       0.052183
```

Estimating Firm-Specific Time-Series Regressions

The price-earnings regressions can also be estimated as firm-specific regressions; that is, the models are estimated for each firm by using the time series of stock prices (or returns) and earnings. This approach yields estimates of the model parameters for each firm in a sample.

Code 7.5: Firm-specific price-earnings regression

```
*** time-series price and return models ;
* select firms with complete time series of earnings data;
proc sort data=windata;
    by firm;
proc means noprint data=windata;
    var eps;
    output out=winbyfirm (drop=_type_ _freq_) n=nobs;
    by firm;
data tswindata;
    merge windata winbyfirm;
    by firm;
    if nobs = 19;

* return model (2b);
proc reg outest=model2b noprint rsquare data=tswindata;
    model anret = defleps;
    by firm;
proc means n mean t prt min max std data=model2b;
    title "mean coefficients of firm-specific return-earnings
regressions";
    var intercept defleps _rsq_;
```

We first sort the data by firms. This is necessary for estimating regressions for each individual firm using a BY statement. A typical problem in this type of research is that we cannot get the required time series of variables for each firm. For instance, the time series of stock price can be relatively short for certain firms because of listings or delistings. To make sure that we have a reasonable amount of observations in time series regressions for each firm, we first determine the lengths of the firm-specific time series and then exclude firms with too few time-series observations.

Accordingly, PROC MEANS calculates the number of observations in the time series of earnings per share for each firm. The N option is used to determine the number of observations in the time series, and results are stored in the variable NOBS and written to the data set WINBYFIRM. The BY statement is needed to perform this procedure for each firm individually.

The data sets WINDATA, which contains the original data, and WINBYFIRM are combined into the new data set TSWINDATA. The IF statement in this DATA step includes only firms that have at least 19 annual observations. Then, as in the cross-sectional approach discussed above, we perform the regressions and average the estimated coefficients. We estimate model (7.2b), in which stock returns are regressed on earnings per share deflated by stock price. Again, you can easily modify the code to estimate the other models.

The results of the firm-specific time-series price-earnings regressions are shown in Output 7.3. The average firm-specific ERC from the return model is 3.570 with a *t*-value of 5.73.

Output 7.3: Results of firm-specific price-earnings regressions

```
         Mean coefficients of firm-specific return-earnings regressions

                             The MEANS Procedure

  Variable   Label       N       Mean   t Value  Pr > |t|      Minimum
  Intercept  Intercept  69   0.9598288    63.13   <.0001     0.3858845
  DEFLEPS               69   3.5703622     5.73   <.0001   -14.4115086
  _RSQ_      R-squared  69   0.0636993     7.99   <.0001   1.0826299E-6


             Variable   Label         Maximum        Std Dev
             Intercept  Intercept   1.3097842      0.1262878
             DEFLEPS               18.5402480      5.1795840
             _RSQ_      R-squared   0.3071249      0.0662648
```

Pooled Time-Series and Cross-Sectional Estimation

In the previous examples, we estimated the price-earnings regressions cross-sectionally (annual regressions) and in time series (firm-specific regressions). The models can also be estimated by pooling the data across firms and years. Next, we briefly illustrate the pooled estimation approach. The simplest way is to estimate the pooled model with OLS, although the estimates will typically be inconsistent.

Code 7.6: Pooled time-series and cross-sectional regressions

```
* pooled ols estimation of price and return model;
proc reg data=windata;
    title "pooled cross-sectional and time-series OLS estimation";
    model anret = defleps / spec acov;
```

PROC REG is used to estimate the earnings response coefficient from model (7.2b) in the same way as in the previous examples. Because we pool the data across firms and years, we need to estimate the model only once. Thus, there is no need to use a BY statement in PROC REG. We use two options to deal with potential heteroscedasticity. First, the SPEC option in the MODEL statement performs White's (1980) test for heteroscedasticity. Second, the ACOV option displays the heteroscedasticity-consistent asymptotic covariance matrix.

Results of the pooled cross-sectional and time-series estimation of the "return" model (7.2b) are shown in Output 7.4. The estimated ERC equals 0.705 with a *t*-value of 4.80. This implies that the relation between stock returns and scaled earnings is significantly positive, but the R^2 is very low (0.007).

Output 7.4: Results of pooled regressions

```
                 Pooled cross-sectional and time-series OLS estimation
                                 The REG Procedure
                                  Model: MODEL1
                            Dependent Variable: ANRET

                                Analysis of Variance

                                      Sum of        Mean
     Source              DF          Squares       Square     F Value    Pr > F
     Model                1          1.87618      1.87618      23.01     <.0001
     Error             3389        276.35220      0.08154
     Corrected Total   3390        278.22838


              Root MSE                  0.28556     R-Square     0.0067
              Dependent Mean            1.06417     Adj R-Sq     0.0065
              Coeff Var                26.83390


                               Parameter Estimates

                          Parameter      Standard
     Variable      DF      Estimate         Error     t Value    Pr > |t|
     Intercept      1       1.04231       0.00669      155.69      <.0001
     DEFLEPS        1       0.70561       0.14710        4.80      <.0001


                 Pooled cross-sectional and time-series OLS estimation
                                 The REG Procedure
                                  Model: MODEL1
                            Dependent Variable: ANRET


                        Consistent Covariance of Estimates

              Variable           Intercept             DEFLEPS
              Intercept       0.0000498174         -0.000742065
              DEFLEPS        -0.000742065           0.0210415166



                         Test of First and Second
                           Moment Specification

                      DF     Chi-Square     Pr > ChiSq
                       2         24.03         <.0001
```

The SPEC option prints White's (1980) χ^2 test for the heteroscedasticity of the model specification.[1] The value of the χ^2 statistic is 24.03 ($p<0.0001$), indicating that the null hypothesis of homoscedasticity can be comfortably rejected. The ACOV option in the MODEL statement prints the asymptotically consistent covariance matrix that allows for heteroscedasticity. These estimates can be used to compute heteroscedasticity-consistent t-statistics. For instance, the variance of the slope of the independent variable DEFLEPS is equal to 0.02104, which means that the standard deviation of DEFLEPS is equal to $(0.02104)^{\frac{1}{2}} =$ 0.1450. The adjusted t-value for DEFLEPS is equal to $0.70548/0.145127 = 4.864$, which is a bit higher than the unadjusted t-value (4.79).

Estimating Price-Earnings Regressions from Panel Data

A more appropriate approach to estimating pooled data is to explicitly model the firm-specific or time-specific effects using panel data. SAS provides several tools to accomplish this; in our example, we use PROC MIXED. It allows data to exhibit correlation and nonconstant variability. The mixed linear model provides the flexibility to model not only the means of your data but also their variances and covariances. Specifically, we re-estimate model (7.2a) and let the intercept and slope coefficient (ERC) vary across firms. This is reasonable given the results from the cross-sectional regressions. We also control for the effect of autocorrelation in the residuals of the model.

Code 7.7: Using PROC MIXED to estimate pooled price-earnings regressions

```
* panel estimation;
proc mixed method=ml data=windata noinfo noitprint noclprint;
    title "price-earnings regressions with firm-varying coefficients and
AR(1) residuals";
    class firm;
    model price = eps / solution;
    random intercept eps / type=un subject=firm solution;
    repeated / type=ar(1)  subject=firm;
quit;
```

The METHOD option in the PROC statement requests maximum likelihood estimation. The remaining options suppress part of the default output for brevity. The CLASS statement informs the procedure that the variable FIRM divides the data into different classes.

As in the PROC REG, the MODEL statement defines the regression model. The SOLUTION option in the MODEL statement requests the fixed-effects coefficient estimates. The RANDOM INTERCEPT EPS statement is then used to relax the assumption of a common intercept and slope coefficient across firms: we now assume that the intercept and slope coefficients across firms follow a bivariate normal distribution. The SOLUTION option again requests the estimated coefficients, and the TYPE and SUBJECT options determine the

---

[1] See H. White, "A Heteroskedasticity-Consistent Covariance Matrix Estimator and a Direct Test for Heteroskedasticity," *Econometrica* (1980) 48: 817-838.

structure of the underlying covariance matrix. Finally, the REPEATED statement instructs the procedure that residuals are autocorrelated within each firm. The results of this estimation are shown in Output 7.5.

Output 7.5: Results of the panel estimation where intercepts and slope coefficients are allowed to vary across firms and annual residuals are allowed to follow AR(1) processes

```
Price-earnings regressions with firm-varying coefficients and AR(1)
residuals
                        The Mixed Procedure


                  Covariance Parameter Estimates
                  Cov Parm      Subject    Estimate
                  UN(1,1)       FIRM         146.46
                  UN(2,1)       FIRM         2.8232
                  UN(2,2)       FIRM         1.7510
                  AR(1)         FIRM         0.5725
                  Residual                   244.54


                        Fit Statistics

             -2 Log Likelihood                27357.4
             AIC (smaller is better)          27371.4
             AICC (smaller is better)         27371.4
             BIC (smaller is better)          27395.5


             Null Model Likelihood Ratio Test
                  DF      Chi-Square       Pr > ChiSq
                  4         2493.69           <.0001


                  Solution for Fixed Effects
                          Standard
       Effect      Estimate      Error      DF      t Value    Pr > |t|
       Intercept    39.5021     0.9873     232       40.01      <.0001
       EPS           2.3014     0.2726     228        8.44      <.0001


                  Solution for Random Effects
                              Std Err
    Effect      FIRM       Estimate      Pred      DF     t Value    Pr > |t|
    Intercept   00195710     2.9317     6.0951    2929      0.48      0.6306
    EPS         00195710     0.3394     1.0760    2929      0.32      0.7524
    Intercept   00282410     5.5060     5.7162    2929      0.96      0.3355
    EPS         00282410     0.1230     1.2863    2929      0.10      0.9238
    Intercept   00790310   -14.8889     7.2952    2929     -2.04      0.0413
    EPS         00790310    -0.5667     1.2183    2929     -0.47      0.6418
    (remaining estimates omitted)
```

Following preliminary information about model and overall fit, the output shows the "Null Model LR Test." This is essentially a test of the null hypothesis that allowing random effects and nonconstant variance does not improve the explanatory power of the model. Because this null is strongly rejected, a fixed-effects model (where coefficients are constant across firms) does not seem appropriate. Next, the section "Solution for Fixed Effects" lists the estimated expectations for the firm-specific intercepts and slopes (recall that we allow the model parameters to vary across firms). The estimated fixed-effect ERC equals 2.301, which is substantially lower than the average ERC from the annual cross-sectional regressions (3.983) reported in Output 7.2. "Solution for Random Effects" presents the firm-specific intercepts and slopes as requested by the RANDOM statement. We find that the estimates vary substantially across firms, although additional testing of the coefficients would be necessary to establish this.

Program Listing

```
* read compustat data from text file;
data cs;
    infile 'c:\comperc.dat';
    input firm $ year eps1 adjfac;
    eps = eps1/adjfac;
    drop eps1 adjfac;

* read crsp data from text file and keep only year-end returns;
data crsp;
    infile 'c:\crsperc.dat';
    input firm $ date yymmdd8. return price mv;
    format date yymmdd6.;
    price = abs(price);
    year = year(date);
    month = month(date);
    if month = 12;
    drop return mv;

* combine compustat and crsp data;
proc sort data=cs;
    by firm year;
proc sort data=crsp;
    by firm date;
data alldata;
    merge cs crsp;
    by firm year;
    lagprice = lag (price);
    lageps   = lag (eps);
    difprice = dif (price);
    difeps   = dif (eps);
    if eps =. or price =. then delete;
```

```
      if first.firm then do;
      lagprice =.; lageps =.; difprice =.; difeps =.;
      end;
      anret    = price  / lagprice;
      defleps  = eps    / lagprice;
      defldif  = difeps / lagprice;
      deflchng = difeps / abs(lageps);

* winsorize earnings and prices, then merge percentiles with data;
proc means noprint data=alldata;
      var price eps difprice difeps anret defleps defldif deflchng;
      output out=extremes (drop=_type_ _freq_)
      p1  = lprice leps ldifpri ldifeps lanret ldefleps ldefldif ldeflchn
      p99 = hprice heps hdifpri hdifeps hanret hdefleps hdefldif hdeflchn;

data windata;
      if _n_=1 then set extremes;
      set alldata;
      if price > hprice or price < lprice then delete;
      if eps > heps or eps < leps then delete;
      if difprice > hdifpri or difprice < ldifpri then delete;
      if difeps > hdifeps or difeps < ldifeps then delete;
      if anret > hanret or anret < lanret then delete;
      if defleps > hdefleps or defleps < ldefleps then delete;
      if defldif > hdefldif or defldif < ldefldif then delete;
      if deflchng > hdeflchn or deflchng < ldeflchn then delete;

proc sort data=windata;
      by year;

* descriptive statistics;
proc means n min mean max std data=windata;
      title "descriptive statistics for winsorized data";
      var price eps difprice difeps anret defleps defldif deflchng;

*** annual price and return models ;
* price model (2a);
proc reg outest=model2a  noprint rsquare data=windata;
      model price = eps / spec;
      by year;
proc means n mean t prt min max std data=model2a;
      title "mean coefficients of annual price-earnings regressions";
      var intercept eps _rsq_;

/* use the commented statements for alternative models
* differenced-price model (2c);
proc reg outest=model2c noprint rsquare data=windata;
      model difprice = difeps ;
      by year;
```

```
proc means n mean t prt min max std data=model2c;
    var intercept difeps _rsq_;

* return model (3a);
proc reg outest=model3a noprint rsquare data=windata;
    model anret = defleps;
    by year;
proc means n mean t prt min max std data=model3a;
    var intercept defleps _rsq_;

* return model (3b);
proc reg outest=model3b noprint rsquare data=windata;
    model anret = defldif;
    by year;
proc means n mean t prt min max std data=model3b;
    var intercept defldif _rsq_;

* return model (3c);
proc reg outest=model3c noprint rsquare data=windata;
    model anret = deflchng;
    by year;
proc means n mean t prt min max std data=model3c;
    var intercept deflchng _rsq_;
*/

*** time-series price and return models ;
* select firms with complete time series of earnings data;
proc sort data=windata;
    by firm;
proc means noprint data=windata;
    var eps;
    output out=winbyfirm (drop=_type_ _freq_) n=nobs;
    by firm;
data tswindata;
    merge windata winbyfirm;
    by firm;
    if nobs = 19;

* return model (2b);
proc reg outest=model2b noprint rsquare data=tswindata;
    model anret = defleps;
    by firm;
proc means n mean t prt min max std data=model2b;
    title "mean coefficients of firm-specific return-earnings
regressions";
    var intercept defleps _rsq_;

* pooled ols estimation of price and return model;
proc reg data=windata;
    title "pooled cross-sectional and time-series ols estimation";
```

```
      model anret = defleps / spec acov;
* panel estimation;
proc mixed method=ml data=windata noinfo noitprint noclprint;
      title "price-earnings regressions with firm-varying coefficients and
ar(1) residuals";
      class firm;
      model price = eps / solution;
      random intercept eps / type=un subject=firm solution;
      repeated / type=ar(1)  subject=firm;
quit;
run;
```

CHAPTER 8

PREDICTING BANKRUPTCY FROM FINANCIAL DISTRESS CHARACTERIZATION MODELS

> **Key Concepts**
> - Discriminant analysis
> - Logit and probit qualitative response models
>
> **Data:** Annual financial statement data

Background for Characterizing Firms in Financial Distress

One of the interesting topics in corporate finance is research concerned with bankruptcy and its prediction. Bankruptcy can result from a firm not being able to make a required bond payment or from a desire by management to restructure its financial obligations. Although bankruptcy itself can have different causes, most cases are preceded by a firm's inability to meet one or more of its financial obligations. Characterizing such financial distress is not only useful for investors in a firm's equity or bond instruments, it is also useful for potential acquiring entities, institutions granting credit or credit ratings, and policy makers.

One problem with characterizing financial distress is that numerous firm-specific variables are potential determinants. Additionally, once analysts make choices as to which variables are important, the question of how to generate a model that effectively classifies a firm as distressed becomes an issue. Numerous variables and methods of analysis have been used in the literature. The seminal article in this branch of literature is probably Altman (1968), whose Z-score model uses liquidity, debt, and operational performance ratios in a discriminant-function framework. A thorough listing of other variables and methods of analysis that have also been used in this literature can be found in Appendix II of Kahya and Theodossiou (1999).

This chapter discusses SAS programs for the three most popular methods of characterizing financial distress: PROC DISCRIM (for discriminant analysis), PROC LOGIT (for logistic qualitative models), and PROC PROBIT (for normally distributed qualitative modeling). The beauty of using SAS for these methods of analysis is the fact that very little programming is required, but a tremendous amount of useful information is generated.

The Data

The data used in this chapter are from Theodossiou, Kahya, Saidi, and Philippatos (1996). In their study, a firm is defined as financially distressed if it meets at least one of the following conditions: (1) actual debt default, (2) management negotiations with creditors to restructure terms of debt instruments, or (3) difficulty in meeting the payment requirements of debt contracts. All data are gathered from Compustat and include only firms listed on NYSE or AMEX from 1981 through 1989. The sample consists of 181 manufacturing firms, of which 86 are classified as financially distressed at some point during this period.[1] Data for the distressed firms are gathered approximately one year prior to exhibiting the first sign of distress. The firm-specific variables used include size measures and ratios measuring liquidity, debt, managerial efficiency, and profitability; they are defined in the following section.

Sample SAS Program to Evaluate Financial Distress Characterization

Reading the Data

The first step is to read the data from a text file. A LABEL statement is included to more easily recognize the variables and output associated with each different method. After reading the data, they are sorted by the distress dummy.

---

[1] The initial sample in Theodossiou, Kahya, Saidi, and Philippatos (1996) includes all financially distressed firms that were delisted between 1981 and 1989 due to acquisition (37 firms) or bankruptcy (44 firms), plus 100 randomly selected firms from the set of all manufacturing firms listed during this period. Five out of the 100 were classified as distressed, so the total set of 181 firms includes 86 distressed firms and 95 healthy firms.

Code 8.1: Read financial statement data and sort by distress status

```
* read data from text file and sort by distress status;
data hwfailed;
     infile 'C:\hwfailed.dat';
     input yd tdta gempl opita invsls lsls lta nwcta cacl qacl ebita reta
fata;
     label        yd     = "Distress Dummy"
                  tdta   = "Debt to Assets"
                  gempl  = "Employee Growth Rate"
                  opita  = "Op. Income to Assets"
                  invsls = "Inventory to Sales"
                  lsls   = "Log of Sales"
                  lta    = "Log of Assets"
                  nwcta  = "Net Working Cap to Assets"
                  cacl   = "Current Assets to Current Liab"
                  qacl   = "Quick Assets to Current Liab"
                  ebita  = "EBIT to Assets"
                  reta   = "Retained Earnings to Assets"
                  ltdta  = "LongTerm Debt to TotAssets"
                  mveltd = "Mkt Value Eqty to LTD"
                  fata   = "Fixed Assets to Assets";

proc sort data=hwfailed;
     by yd;
```

We use the following variables:

```
YD        The distress dummy, which equals 1 for distress and 0 for
          healthy firm
TDTA      The firm's debt-to-total assets ratio
GEMPL     The firm's one-year employee growth rate
OPITA     The firm's operating income-to-assets ratio
INVSLS    The firm's inventory-to-sales ratio
LSLS      The log of a firm's sales
LTA       The log of a firm's total assets
NWCTA     The firm's net working capital-to-total assets ratio
CACL      The firm's current assets-to-current liabilities ratio
QACL      The firm's quick assets-to-current liabilities
EBITA     The firm's earnings before interest and taxes-to-total assets ratio
RETA      The firm's retained earnings-to-total assets ratio
LTDTA     Long-term debt divided by total assets
MVELTD    Market value of equity divided by long-term debt
FATA      The firm's fixed assets-to-total assets ratio
```

The variables used to characterize financial distress originate from numerous traditional accounting ratios and measures of firm size. The accounting ratios cover liquidity, debt, managerial effectiveness, and profitability measures. Each measure has been shown to have some relevance for characterizing financial distress in different studies. Again, see Appendix II of Kahya and Theodossiou (1999) for a detailed listing of which articles introduced which variables.

Because the purpose of this analysis is to gauge the efficacy of financial characteristics in classifying firms in financial distress, the data are sorted based on the financial distress classification. That is, the purpose of the analysis is to determine whether the financial ratios or variables can help determine whether a firm is classified as either a YD = 0 or a YD = 1.

Univariate Analysis

First, we would like to get an indication of whether there are differences between the financial variables across the two samples. Although not a descriptive model per se, PROC TTEST can be used to identify statistically significant differences of means on a univariate basis. We use it here to test whether some of the variables are different for distressed firms.

Code 8.2: Univariate analysis of the determinants of financial distress

```
proc ttest data=hwfailed;
    title "univariate analysis of distress characteristics";
    class yd;
```

The CLASS statement instructs the procedure to evaluate the difference in means between financially distressed firms (*yd=1*) and those classified as not being in distress (*yd=0*). The output of this procedure is listed next.

Output 8.1: Univariate analysis of the determinants of financial distress

```
            univariate analysis of distress characteristics
                        The TTEST Procedure

                            Statistics
```

Variable	yd		N	Lower CL Mean	Mean	Upper CL Mean	Lower CL Std Dev	Std Dev
tdta		0	95	0.4382	0.4694	0.5007	0.1342	0.1534
tdta		1	86	0.6055	0.6578	0.7101	0.2122	0.244
tdta	Diff (1-2)			-0.248	-0.188	-0.129	0.1827	0.2016
gempl		0	95	0.0092	0.0303	0.0514	0.0906	0.1036
gempl		1	86	-0.057	-0.035	-0.013	0.0873	0.1003
gempl	Diff (1-2)			0.0353	0.0653	0.0953	0.0925	0.102
opita		0	95	0.1398	0.1578	0.1757	0.077	0.088

Output 8.1 (continued)

opita		1	86	0.0285	0.056	0.0836	0.1116	0.1284
opita	Diff (1-2)			0.0697	0.1017	0.1337	0.0988	0.109
invsls		0	95	0.1409	0.1567	0.1724	0.0677	0.0773
invsls		1	86	0.1673	0.1923	0.2173	0.1015	0.1167
invsls	Diff (1-2)			-0.064	-0.036	-0.007	0.0888	0.098
lsls		0	95	5.6168	5.974	6.3312	1.5345	1.7533
lsls		1	86	5.1435	5.4575	5.7716	1.2739	1.4649
lsls	Diff (1-2)			0.0399	0.5165	0.9931	1.4707	1.6228
lta		0	95	5.2272	5.5855	5.9438	1.5394	1.7589
lta		1	86	4.7916	5.1208	5.45	1.3354	1.5355
lta	Diff (1-2			-0.022	0.4647	0.9512	1.5013	1.6566
nwcta		0	95	0.2601	0.2939	0.3277	0.1454	0.1661
nwcta		1	86	0.205	0.2452	0.2855	0.1633	0.1878
nwcta	Diff (1-2)			-0.003	0.0487	0.1006	0.1602	0.1767
cacl		0	95	2.1718	2.3945	2.6171	0.9567	1.0931
cacl		1	86	1.8061	2.0256	2.245	0.8901	1.0236
cacl	Diff (1-2)			0.0574	0.3689	0.6804	0.9612	1.0606
qacl		0	95	1.1907	1.3778	1.5649	0.8037	0.9183
qacl		1	86	0.9647	1.133	1.3012	0.6825	0.7848
qacl	Diff (1-2)			-0.007	0.2448	0.4967	0.7771	0.8575
ebita		0	95	0.093	0.1126	0.1322	0.0841	0.0961
ebita		1	86	-0.014	0.0146	0.0435	0.1172	0.1347
ebita	Diff (1-2)			0.0639	0.098	0.1321	0.1052	0.1161
reta		0	95	0.3204	0.3577	0.395	0.1603	0.1832
reta		1	86	0.0637	0.1323	0.2008	0.2779	0.3196
reta	Diff (1-2)			0.1499	0.2255	0.301	0.233	0.2571
ltdta		0	95	-4.877	-1.932	1.0128	12.653	14.457
ltdta		1	86	0.1859	0.2211	0.2564	0.143	0.1644
ltdta	Diff (1-2)			-5.23	-2.153	0.9239	9.4949	10.477
mveltd		0	95	-0.667	1.6654	3.9982	10.023	11.451
mveltd		1	86	0.6925	0.9682	1.2438	1.1182	1.2858
mveltd	Diff (1-2)			-1.754	0.6972	3.1485	7.5634	8.3457
fata		0	95	0.3303	0.3649	0.3995	0.1486	0.1698
fata		1	86	0.2793	0.3127	0.3462	0.1357	0.156
fata	Diff (1-2)			0.0042	0.0522	0.1002	0.1481	0.1634

Statistics

Variable	yd		Upper CL Std Dev	Std Err	Minimum	Maximum
tdta		0	0.1789	0.0157	0.1455	0.7997
tdta		1	0.2871	0.0263	0.1083	1.513
tdta	Diff (1-2)		0.2249	0.03		
gempl		0	0.1208	0.0106	-0.273	0.4565
gempl		1	0.1181	0.0108	-0.288	0.3529
gempl	Diff (1-2)		0.1138	0.0152		
opita		0	0.1027	0.009	-0.184	0.3822
opita		1	0.151	0.0138	-0.4	0.3668
opita	Diff (1-2)		0.1216	0.0162		
invsls		0	0.0902	0.0079	0.0163	0.3938
invsls		1	0.1373	0.0126	0.0348	0.8367
invsls	Diff (1-2)		0.1093	0.0146		
lsls		0	2.0455	0.1799	2.2434	11.379

Output 8.1 (continued)

lsls		1	1.7237	0.158	2.1923	10.01
lsls	Diff (1-2)		1.8102	0.2415		
lta		0	2.0519	0.1805	1.9689	11.017
lta		1	1.8068	0.1656	1.7032	9.5025
lta	Diff (1-2)		1.848	0.2466		
nwcta		0	0.1937	0.017	-0.007	0.7936
nwcta		1	0.221	0.0202	-0.429	0.7145
nwcta	Diff (1-2)		0.1971	0.0263		
cacl		0	1.2752	0.1121	0.9372	6.4528
cacl		1	1.2045	0.1104	0.4788	6.8381
cacl	Diff (1-2)		1.1832	0.1579		
qacl		0	1.0713	0.0942	0.2217	6.0934
qacl		1	0.9235	0.0846	0.1227	5.3057
qacl	Diff (1-2)		0.9566	0.1276		
ebita		0	0.1121	0.0099	-0.357	0.2845
ebita		1	0.1585	0.0145	-0.482	0.3102
ebita	Diff (1-2)		0.1295	0.0173		
reta		0	0.2137	0.0188	0.0069	0.8352
reta		1	0.3761	0.0345	-0.959	0.7725
reta	Diff (1-2)		0.2868	0.0383		
ltdta		0	16.865	1.4832	-99.99	0.5661
ltdta		1	0.1935	0.0177	0	0.902
ltdta	Diff (1-2)		11.687	1.5594		
mveltd		0	13.359	1.1749	-99.99	27.632
mveltd		1	1.513	0.1387	0.053	6.5552
mveltd	Diff (1-2)		9.3098	1.2422		
fata		0	0.1981	0.0174	0.0272	0.805
fata		1	0.1836	0.0168	0.032	0.6488
fata	Diff (1-2)		0.1823	0.0243		

T-Tests

Variable	Method	Variances	DF	t Value	Pr > |t|
tdta	Pooled	Equal	179	-6.28	<.0001
tdta	Satterthwaite	Unequal	140	-6.14	<.0001
gempl	Pooled	Equal	179	4.30	<.0001
gempl	Satterthwaite	Unequal	178	4.31	<.0001
opita	Pooled	Equal	179	6.27	<.0001
opita	Satterthwaite	Unequal	148	6.15	<.0001
invsls	Pooled	Equal	179	-2.44	0.0155
invsls	Satterthwaite	Unequal	145	-2.40	0.0178
lsls	Pooled	Equal	179	2.14	0.0338
lsls	Satterthwaite	Unequal	178	2.16	0.0323
lta	Pooled	Equal	179	1.88	0.0611
lta	Satterthwaite	Unequal	179	1.90	0.0594
nwcta	Pooled	Equal	179	1.85	0.0659
nwcta	Satterthwaite	Unequal	171	1.84	0.0677
cacl	Pooled	Equal	179	2.34	0.0206
cacl	Satterthwaite	Unequal	179	2.34	0.0202
qacl	Pooled	Equal	179	1.92	0.0567

Output 8.1 (continued)

qacl	Satterthwaite	Unequal	178	1.93	0.0548
ebita	Pooled	Equal	179	5.67	<.0001
ebita	Satterthwaite	Unequal	152	5.58	<.0001
reta	Pooled	Equal	179	5.89	<.0001
reta	Satterthwaite	Unequal	132	5.74	<.0001
ltdta	Pooled	Equal	179	-1.38	0.1690
ltdta	Satterthwaite	Unequal	94	-1.45	0.1499
mveltd	Pooled	Equal	179	0.56	0.5753
mveltd	Satterthwaite	Unequal	96.6	0.59	0.5570
fata	Pooled	Equal	179	2.15	0.0333
fata	Satterthwaite	Unequal	179	2.15	0.0325

Equality of Variances

Variable	Method	Num DF	Den DF	F Value	Pr > F
tdta	Folded F	85	94	2.53	<.0001
gempl	Folded F	94	85	1.07	0.7690
opita	Folded F	85	94	2.13	0.0004
invsls	Folded F	85	94	2.28	<.0001
lsls	Folded F	94	85	1.43	0.0929
lta	Folded F	94	85	1.31	0.2036
nwcta	Folded F	85	94	1.28	0.2453
cacl	Folded F	94	85	1.14	0.5390
qacl	Folded F	94	85	1.37	0.1416
ebita	Folded F	85	94	1.96	0.0015
reta	Folded F	85	94	3.04	<.0001
ltdta	Folded F	94	85	7732.37	<.0001
mveltd	Folded F	94	85	79.32	<.0001
fata	Folded F	94	85	1.18	0.4278

The output from PROC TTEST can be broken into three distinct sections. The first generates statistical summary information for each variable. Each of the statistics is computed for both levels of the classification variable. A useful piece of information is the difference between classification levels. For instance, examine the statistical information generated for the total debt-to-total assets ratio, TDTA. We have 95 observations in the "healthy firm" classification and 86 observations in the "distressed" classification. Healthy firms have an average TDTA of approximately 47%, while for distressed firms it is about 66%. The difference is about 19%, which can be read directly from the "Diff (1-2)" row. Hence, distressed firms appear to have higher debt ratios than those classified as not in distress.

The second section generated by PROC TTEST is the main output of interest: the statistical differences between the means across the two groups. Two *t*-tests are calculated; one assumes equal variances between the two classes, and the other assumes unequal variances. We find that all test statistics, except for the debt-to-asset and equity-to-debt ratios (LTDTA and MVELTD), are statistically significant at least at the 10% level (most variables at lower levels). This implies that most variables have statistically different means between healthy and distressed firms.

The third section contains test statistics for the null hypothesis that the variance across groups are equal. These tests help us to choose between the two reported *t*-tests in the previous section. For example, if the null of equal variance is rejected at a reasonable level, then we should not draw inferences from the two-sample *t*-test assuming equal variances. Instead, in those cases, the *t*-test assuming unequal variances seems the better choice. In our sample, eight variables appear to have significantly different variances at the 10% level or better.

So far, the univariate results indicate that a large number of the financial variables are different between distressed and healthy firms. However, this analysis does not take into account interactions between those variables. Therefore, we consider different multivariate methods next.

Discriminant Analysis

PROC DISCRIM helps generate classification schemes using discriminant analysis. This method uses multiple variables as inputs to classify each observation into one or more groupings. When the analyst has identified whether the sample firms are distressed or healthy, discriminant analysis may help to characterize the classifications. PROC DISCRIM generates a discriminant function and calculates error rates regarding group classification. These error rates can then be used to compare whether certain variables are better than others in identifying distressed firms. Next, we use PROC DISCRIM to relate the variables discussed earlier in this chapter to the classification of a firm as distressed or healthy.

Code 8.3: Discriminant analysis

```
proc discrim data=hwfailed;
    title "discriminant analysis of distress characteristics";
    class yd;
```

Again, the CLASS statement is used to tell the procedure which variable contains the classification. Because no VAR statement is used, the procedure uses all numeric variables in the input data set (except those listed in the CLASS statement). This generates the following output.

Output 8.2: Discriminant analysis

```
              discriminant analysis of distress characteristics
                        The DISCRIM Procedure

        Observations       181         DF Total              180
        Variables           12         DF Within Classes     179
        Classes              2         DF Between Classes      1

                        Class Level Information
              Variable                                          Prior
      yd      Name      Frequency      Weight    Proportion    Probability
       0       _0            95       95.0000     0.524862      0.500000
       1       _1            86       86.0000     0.475138      0.500000
```

Output 8.2 (continued)

```
                    Pooled Covariance Matrix Information
                              Natural Log of the
                  Covariance      Determinant of the
                  Matrix Rank      Covariance Matrix
                       14              -32.55611

          Pairwise Generalized Squared Distances Between Groups
                    2       _    _    -1   _    _
                   D (i|j) = (X - X )' COV   (X - X )
                              i   j          i   j

                   Generalized Squared Distance to yd
                From yd             0               1
                      0             0          1.92349
                      1        1.92349               0

                      Linear Discriminant Function
                            -1  _                              -1  _
          Constant = -.5 X' COV  X       Coefficient Vector = COV   X
                        j      j                                    j


                   Linear Discriminant Function for yd
```

Variable	Label	0	1
Constant		-53.74891	-54.53513
tdta	Debt to Assets	74.33226	77.46389
gempl	Employee Growth Rate	4.73280	-1.58254
opita	Op. Income to Assets	65.90113	49.87403
invsls	Inventory to Sales	68.27129	73.73180
lsls	Log of Sales	10.94297	10.93718
lta	Log of Assets	-9.15723	-9.27636
nwcta	Net Working Cap to Assets	19.14528	18.51582
cacl	Current Assets to Current Liab	-3.70633	-4.41209
qacl	Quick Assets to Current Liab	14.71980	15.95579
ebita	EBIT to Assets	-65.57783	-53.64473
reta	Retained Earnings to Assets	42.61724	41.82193
ltdta	LongTerm Debt to TotAssets	-0.07422	-0.05404
mveltd	Mkt Value Eqty to LTD	-0.08401	-0.09766
fata	Fixed Assets to Assets	33.55732	33.81346

```
         Classification Summary for Calibration Data: WORK.HWFAILED
            Resubstitution Summary using Linear Discriminant Function

                   Generalized Squared Distance Function
                    2         _    -1   _
                   D (X) = (X-X )' COV  (X-X )
                    j       j          j
```

Output 8.2 (continued)

```
          Posterior Probability of Membership in Each yd
                          2                        2
         Pr(j|X) = exp(-.5 D (X)) / SUM exp(-.5 D (X))
                          j        k        k

       Number of Observations and Percent Classified into yd
          From yd          0            1          Total
             0             78           17           95
                        82.11        17.89       100.00


             1             28           58           86
                        32.56        67.44       100.00


          Total          106           75          181
                        58.56        41.44       100.00


       Priors            0.5          0.5

               Error Count Estimates for yd
                          0            1          Total
          Rate        0.1789       0.3488       0.2639
          Priors      0.5000       0.5000
```

The output from PROC DISCRIM offers useful information regarding the data—especially classification information. The first output section lists general characteristics of the data, such as the number of observations, the number of observations per class level, and the proportion of observations in each level.

The second section starts by describing the generalized squared distance between groups. Because our example involves only two groups, we cannot judge whether 1.92349 signifies much. Next, it describes the linear discriminant function, which lists the classification scheme weightings for each variable. The larger the difference for a variable across class levels, the better this variable is suited as a predictor of distress. Finally, the information that tells us the most relates to the error rates generated by the linear discriminant model. For instance, out of the 95 healthy firms, the linear discriminant classification classifies 17 as distressed. Hence, the error rate for healthy firms is approximately 18%. Out of the 86 distressed firms, 30 are classified as healthy. This corresponds to an error rate of about 35%. Overall, 47 out of 181 firms are classified incorrectly, resulting in an overall error rate of 26%. Thus, 74% are classified correctly, which seems to be an improvement over a naive prior of 50%. To get a better impression of the predictive ability of this analysis, however, it would be important to perform an out-of-sample test.

Although PROC DISCRIM may be useful to identify distressed firms, the model has little to say about the statistical power of its classification. We now turn to more statistically rigorous methods, logit and probit, that can also be used to test hypotheses about the determinants of distress.

Qualitative Response Models

Both logit and probit models can be used to analyze the determinants of qualitative response variables. In our example, the response is the distress dummy YD that classifies each sample firm either as distressed or as healthy. We are now interested in how each of the variables affects the probability of distress. Both logit and probit model the probability of a certain response (in this case, one or zero) as a function of the independent variables. Both assume that the underlying response is unobservable, and that only the qualitative response (here, one or zero) can be observed. The two methods then differ in their respective assumptions about how the observed dummy variable is related to the unobservable true response. Logit assumes that the true response is a linear function of the independent variables plus a logistic error term, while probit assumes a normally distributed error term.

The coefficients of both models are estimated using maximum likelihood. Although the estimated coefficients are not probability measures, they do show whether an independent variable is positively or negatively related to the probability (of distress, in our case).

To continue our example, we now apply PROC LOGIT and PROC PROBIT to our sample. For brevity, we include only the variables that were most significant in Theodossiou, Kahya, Saidi, and Philippatos's (1996) study.

Code 8.4: Logit and probit models to explain financial distress

```
proc logistic data=hwfailed;
    title "logistic analysis of distress characteristics";
    model yd = tdta gempl opita invsls lsls /rsquare;

proc probit data=hwfailed;
    title "probit analysis of distress characteristics";
    class yd;
    model yd = tdta gempl opita invsls lsls;
```

The output of each procedure is shown below.

Output 8.3: Logit and probit models to explain financial distress

```
            logistic analysis of distress characteristics
                     The LOGISTIC Procedure

                         Model Information

    Data Set                    WORK.HWFAILED
    Response Variable           yd                      Distress Dummy
    Number of Response Levels   2
    Number of Observations      181
    Link Function               Logit
    Optimization Technique      Fisher's scoring
```

Output 8.3 (continued)

```
                        Response Profile
                Ordered                      Total
                 Value         yd          Frequency
                   1            0              95
                   2            1              86
                   Model Convergence Status
            Convergence criterion (GCONV=1E-8) satisfied.

                      Model Fit Statistics
                                            Intercept
                                 Intercept     and
               Criterion           Only     Covariates
               AIC                252.472     193.113
               SC                 255.670     212.304
               -2 Log L           250.472     181.113


           R-Square     0.3183    Max-rescaled R-Square    0.4248

                Testing Global Null Hypothesis: BETA=0
           Test                Chi-Square      DF     Pr > ChiSq
           Likelihood Ratio      69.3590        5       <.0001
           Score                 53.5591        5       <.0001
           Wald                  36.2002        5       <.0001

              Analysis of Maximum Likelihood Estimates
                                 Standard
         Parameter    DF    Estimate     Error    Chi-Square    Pr > ChiSq
         Intercept    1      1.5085      1.0436      2.0893        0.1483
         tdta         1     -4.8126      1.2170     15.6382        <.0001
         gempl        1      6.1221      1.9810      9.5502        0.0020
         opita        1      5.1422      2.3576      4.7573        0.0292
         invsls       1     -3.6196      2.3606      2.3510        0.1252
         lsls         1      0.2151      0.1251      2.9550        0.0856


                       Odds Ratio Estimates


                         Point           95% Wald
            Effect      Estimate      Confidence Limits
            tdta         0.008       <0.001       0.088
            gempl      455.799        9.387     >999.999
            opita      171.098        1.684     >999.999
            invsls       0.027       <0.001       2.738
            lsls         1.240        0.970       1.585
```

Output 8.3 (continued)

```
            Association of Predicted Probabilities and Observed Responses
                  Percent Concordant      83.0    Somers' D    0.662
                  Percent Discordant      16.8    Gamma        0.663
                  Percent Tied             0.1    Tau-a        0.332
                  Pairs                   8170    c            0.831


                       probit analysis of distress characteristics
                                Probit Procedure

                            Class Level Information
                       Name       Levels    Values
                       yd              2     0 1

                             Model Information

        Data Set                     WORK.HWFAILED
        Dependent Variable                     yd    Distress Dummy
        Number of Observations                181
        Name of Distribution               NORMAL
        Log Likelihood             -90.28587843

                             Response Profile
                        Level          Count
                        0                 95
                        1                 86

  Algorithm converged.

                          Goodness-of-Fit Tests

         Statistic                       Value       DF    Pr > ChiSq
         Pearson Chi-Square            161.7394      175       0.7554
         L.R.    Chi-Square            180.5718      175       0.3706

                        Response-Covariate Profile
                        Response Levels                  2
                        Number of Covariate Values     181

  Since the chi-square is small (p > 0.1000), fiducial limits will be
  calculated using a t value of  1.96.
```

Output 8.3 (continued)

```
              Analysis of Parameter Estimates
                          Standard
    Variable   DF   Estimate     Error Chi-Square Pr > ChiSq
    Intercept  1    0.99737    0.60556    2.7127    0.0996
    tdta       1   -2.92789    0.70270   17.3607   <.0001
    gempl      1    3.74718    1.18885    9.9346    0.0016
    opita      1    2.86128    1.32298    4.6775    0.0306
    invsls     1   -2.24802    1.40335    2.5661    0.1092
    lsls       1    0.12505    0.07382    2.8694    0.0903


              Analysis of Parameter
                    Estimates


          Variable   Label

          Intercept  Intercept
          tdta       Debt to Assets
          gempl      Employee Growth Rate
          opita      Op. Income to Assets
          invsls     Inventory to Sales
          lsls       Log of Sales
```

The PROC LOGIT results indicate the following. First, an approximate R^2, termed the "Max-rescaled R-Square," of 42% is reported (note that this is not a good measure of fit for maximum-likelihood estimations). All three tests of the null hypothesis that all coefficients jointly equal zero—the likelihood ratio test, the score test, and the Wald test—imply that the model has significant explanatory power. Of the five independent variables, TDTA, GEMPL, OPITA, INVSLS, and LSLS, the first three are significant at the 5% level or better.

To interpret the estimated coefficients it is important that, by default, PROC LOGIT models the probability of the smallest class level. In this case, this is the value zero that indicates a healthy firm. Thus, increasing values of a variable that has a significantly positive coefficient make it more likely that the firm is healthy, and vice versa. For the sample analyzed in this chapter, the signs of the estimates make intuitive sense. For example, TDTA has a significant negative coefficient. This implies that, controlling for changes in the other four variables, a larger total debt-to-total assets ratio lowers the probability that a firm will be classified as healthy. The other two significant coefficients on employee growth and operating income-to-total assets are positive, implying that an increase will also increase the likelihood of being healthy.

The "Association of Predicted Probabilities and Observed Responses" output section indicates that logit has correctly classified approximately 84% of the observations, which appears to be an improvement over the 75% success rate with the discriminant analysis. The probit results largely agree with the logit ones, but the model's explanatory power is not significant. Nevertheless, the signs of the estimated coefficients are the same as those in the logit estimation.

Summary

The purpose of this chapter was to illustrate how to use SAS to characterize the determinants of financial distress. We presented three common methods: discriminant, logit, and probit analysis. Discriminant analysis helps generate direct links between variables and classifications, but does not allow much hypothesis testing. Both logit and probit, on the other hand, allow hypothesis testing, but depend on distributional assumptions about the error term.

Program Listing

```
* read data from text file and sort by distress status;
data hwfailed;
     infile 'C:\hwfailed.dat';
     input yd tdta gempl opita invsls lsls lta nwcta cacl qacl ebita reta
fata;
     label     yd      = "Distress Dummy"
               tdta    = "Debt to Assets"
               gempl   = "Employee Growth Rate"
               opita   = "Op. Income to Assets"
               invsls  = "Inventory to Sales"
               lsls    = "Log of Sales"
               lta     = "Log of Assets"
               nwcta   = "Net Working Cap to Assets"
               cacl    = "Current Assets to Current Liab"
               qacl    = "Quick Assets to Current Liab"
               ebita   = "EBIT to Assets"
               reta    = "Retained Earnings to Assets"
               ltdta   = "LongTerm Debt to TotAssets"
               mveltd  = "Mkt Value Eqty to LTD"
               fata    = "Fixed Assets to Assets";

proc sort data=hwfailed;
     by yd;

proc ttest data=hwfailed;
     title "univariate analysis of distress characteristics";
     class yd;
```

```
proc discrim data=hwfailed;
    title "discriminant analysis of distress characteristics";
    class yd;

proc logistic data=hwfailed;
    title "logistic analysis of distress characteristics";
    model yd = tdta gempl opita invsls lsls /rsquare;

proc probit data=hwfailed;
    title "probit analysis of distress characteristics";
    class yd;
    model yd = tdta gempl opita invsls lsls;
run;
```

CHAPTER 9

USING ACCOUNTING INFORMATION TO FORECAST MARKET PERFORMANCE

> **Key Concepts**
> - Grouping stocks into earnings-price and book-to-market quintiles
> - Computing correlations
>
> **Data:** Annual stock returns and financial statement variables

Background for Analyzing Fundamental Accounting Information and Market Performance

This chapter discusses the cross-sectional relationships between fundamental accounting ratios and stock returns. Accounting variables, such as the book value of equity and earnings information, have long been used in the financial community to assist in making investment decisions. Financial statement variables are easy to collect and implicitly represent a connection between operating performance and valuation. Not only have accounting variables been of interest to the practicing financial analyst and portfolio manager, but the relationship between these variables and stock performance has also been of interest to the financial market researcher.

Numerous research efforts have investigated the relationship between the book value-to-market value ratio (B/M) and the earnings-to-price ratio (E/P) to stock returns. These efforts allow inferences on the return performance of two popular investment styles, value vs. growth. Low B/M and E/P firms are classified as "growth" or "glamour" companies, whereas high B/M and E/P firms are classified as "value " firms.

The results of numerous studies indicate that value investing outperforms growth investing. Basu (1977), Lakonishok, Shleifer, and Vishny (1994), and Haugen (1995) are examples that show value stocks outperforming growth stocks, even over long investment horizons up to five years. The connection between the accounting data driven ratios and stock performance has been linked to growth prospects of the firms. Value stock ratios indicate low growth prospects, and those firms whose stocks are classified as growth or glamour stocks point toward high future growth forecasts. It is often argued, as by Lakonishok, Shleifer, and Vishny (1994), that the expectations for glamour firms to meet those growth forecasts are also high, so when disappointments occur, the price impact on glamour firms is especially devastating. On the other hand, growth expectations for value firms are somewhat low, so when these firms do better than expected, the appreciation in stock price is forthcoming. Hence, the investment performance advantage of value stocks over growth stocks is clear.

Not only do fundamental ratios appear important in analyzing the performance aspect of value vs. growth firms, but Fama and French (1992) indicate that the ratios may also be important for capital asset pricing models. Specifically, the B/M ratio and firm size appear to be important variables that compete with CAPM frameworks. In this case it is argued that the covariance with the market portfolio alone does not fully account for priced firm risk. That is, the easily generated B/M ratio may contain a measure of risk that is important to investors and priced in the market, which translates into the noted statistical significance found by Fama and French (1992).

The Data

The data used in this chapter are part of the data analyzed in Broussard, Michayluk, and Neely (2000) and are collected from Compustat. Additionally, information on return and market value comes from CRSP. Portfolios are created three months after the end of each firm's fiscal year and are held for five years without rebalancing. We form quintile portfolios based on the B/M and E/P ratios to examine the impact these fundamental financial variables have on returns. The SAS program for this analysis is discussed in the following section.

Sample Program to Evaluate Fundamental Financial Information and Market Performance

The first step is to read the data from a text file. The DATA step assumes that Compustat and CRSP data have already been merged into one file.

Code 9.1: Read data

```
* read crsp and compustat data;
data base;
    infile 'C:\newcrsp.output';
    input cusip $ @10 psdate yymmdd8. @28 hpr5yr @39 price @50 eps @63 bm
@154 mktval;
    format psdate yymmdd6.;
    ep = eps/price;
    yy = year(psdate);
    if bm < 0 then bm = .;
    * keep only records with data for both crsp & compustat;
    if ep = . then delete;
    * labels;
    label hpr5yr = '5yr holding period return';
    label ep = 'earnings-to-price ratio';
    label bm = 'book-to-market ratio';
    label mktval = 'market value of equity';
    label price = 'share price';
    * variable selection;
    keep cusip psdate pedate hpr5yr price ep bm mktval yy;
```

The variables are described in the LABEL statements. Additionally, we extract the year YY from the portfolio-formation date PSDATE. Note that we use line-pointer controls to read from the input file. In this case, the input file contains additional variables that we do not need for the sample program. The line pointers are used to skip these unnecessary fields. Each pointer "@N" tells the INPUT statement to begin reading the next variable at column N in the input file. Next, we use PROC CORR to analyze the correlations between these variables.

Code 9.2: Compute correlations among analysis variables

```
proc corr data=base;
    title 'correlation analysis of relevant variables';
    var hpr5yr ep bm mktval price;
```

Output 9.1: Correlation analysis of five-year-ahead returns and other variables

```
           correlation analysis of relevant variables
                       The CORR Procedure

     5  Variables:     hpr5yr    ep        bm        mktval    price

                          Simple Statistics

       Variable          N         Mean        Std Dev          Sum
       hpr5yr         7932      1.15231        1.72352         9140
       ep             7932      0.31782       19.96877         2521
       bm             7932      2.34915       56.45280        18633
       mktval         7932         1414           4106     11215678
       price          7932     33.01632      148.77751       261885

                          Simple Statistics

             Variable      Minimum        Maximum
             hpr5yr       -0.91574       43.12303
             ep          0.0002504           1778
             bm           0.00100           3728
             mktval       0.22700          93236
             price        0.03662           8025

                Pearson Correlation Coefficients, N = 7932
                    Prob > |r| under H0: Rho=0

              hpr5yr            ep            bm        mktval         price
   hpr5yr    1.00000      -0.00388       0.00528      -0.01853       0.01204
                            0.7294        0.6381        0.0989        0.2838


   ep       -0.00388       1.00000      -0.00035      -0.00059      -0.00269
             0.7294                       0.9751        0.9578        0.8106


   bm        0.00528      -0.00035       1.00000      -0.01083      -0.00017
             0.6381        0.9751                       0.3348        0.9876


   mktval   -0.01853      -0.00059      -0.01083       1.00000       0.08920
             0.0989        0.9578        0.3348                       <.0001


   price     0.01204      -0.00269      -0.00017       0.08920       1.00000
             0.2838        0.8106        0.9876        <.0001
```

In this output, we have omitted the variable labels to conserve space. The results show little correlation between the five-year holding period returns and the other variables. The only variable that shows a marginally significant correlation with the five-year holding period return is MKTVAL (the firm's market value). This result is consistent with a size effect in this data, which has characterized U.S. stock returns for most of the 20th century: smaller firms have higher five-year holding period returns. It is also important for our subsequent analysis that BM and EP are not related. Therefore, separate rankings by these two variables should produce outcomes that are independent.

Now that we have gathered some simple correlations, we will generate additional statistics for the earnings-to-price and book-to-market portfolios. We employ PROC RANK to create quintiles annually based on the E/P and B/M ratios.

Code 9.3: Create quintiles for earnings-to-price and book-to-market ratios

```
* sort by year and create annual quintiles for ep;
proc sort data=base;
    by yy;
proc rank data=base groups=5 out=baseranks;
    var   ep  bm  mktval   price;
    ranks rank_ep rank_bm rank_mktval rank_price;
    by yy;
```

PROC RANK reads the data set BASE and creates new variables that correspond to the ranks of the four variables listed in the VAR statement. Because we need quintiles, the groups statement instructs the procedure to first arrange the data into five (about) equally sized sorted groups and then record the corresponding rank for each observation. The new data set BASERANKS contains the input data and additionally four new rank variables as requested in the RANKS statement. For example, the new variable RANK_EP contains the rank of the associated EP quintile (values range from 0 to 4).

Code 9.4: Univariate analysis of portfolios ranked by the earnings-to-price ratio

```
* univariate analysis of earnings-to-price portfolios;
proc sort data=baseranks;
    by rank_ep;
proc means data=baseranks n mean std cv;
    title 'univariate analysis of earnings-to-price portfolios';
    by rank_ep;
    var ep bm hpr5yr rank_mktval rank_price;
proc anova data=baseranks;
    class rank_ep;
    model hpr5yr = rank_ep;
    quit;
```

Now we perform an univariate analysis of mean returns for each earnings-price quintile. The data are first sorted by the ranking variable, and then PROC MEANS is used to produce descriptive statistics. To test the hypothesis that returns are equal across earnings-price quintiles, we use PROC ANOVA. It performs a simple analysis of variance and tests whether the analysis variable HPR5YR is equal across the levels of the classification variable RANK_EP. The output from this step is shown below.

Output 9.2: Earnings-to-price portfolios

```
            univariate analysis of earnings-to-price portfolios

----------------------------- rank_ep=0 --------------------------------

                           The MEANS Procedure

                                                           Coeff of
     Variable        N          Mean        Std Dev       Variation
     ep            1583     0.0350921      0.0141653      40.3661529
     bm            1583     4.9217852    110.7548049       2250.30
     hpr5yr        1583     1.0826778      1.8856423     174.1646670
     rank_mktval   1583     1.9437776      1.4429733      74.2355151
     rank_price    1583     1.8553380      1.5063860      81.1919991

----------------------------- rank_ep=1 --------------------------------
                                                           Coeff of
     Variable        N          Mean        Std Dev       Variation
     ep            1589     0.0599007      0.0087970      14.6859029
     bm            1589     0.8397823      6.7978737     809.4805143
     hpr5yr        1589     1.0622880      1.5941576     150.0682998
     rank_mktval   1589     2.2806797      1.3398600      58.7482750
     rank_price    1589     2.2498427      1.4061337      62.4991997

----------------------------- rank_ep=2 --------------------------------
                                                           Coeff of
     Variable        N          Mean        Std Dev       Variation
     ep            1586     0.0757654      0.0106908      14.1103394
     bm            1586     0.8833436      2.7337986     309.4830221
     hpr5yr        1586     1.1260081      1.5572198     138.2956118
     rank_mktval   1586     2.0315259      1.3462001      66.2654673
     rank_price    1586     2.1336696      1.3966300      65.4567144
```

Output 9.2 (continued)

```
------------------------------ rank_ep=3 -------------------------------
                                                          Coeff of
    Variable        N          Mean         Std Dev      Variation
    ep            1588       0.0938230     0.0134788     14.3662306
    bm            1588       1.4626914    12.2638884    838.4467254
    hpr5yr        1588       1.1223828     1.5064470    134.2186449
    rank_mktval   1588       1.9382872     1.4030195     72.3845044
    rank_price    1588       2.0623426     1.3265806     64.3239687

------------------------------ rank_ep=4 -------------------------------
                                                          Coeff of
    Variable        N          Mean         Std Dev      Variation
    ep            1586       1.3247623    44.6542009      3370.73
    bm            1586       3.6470063    59.0370093      1618.78
    hpr5yr        1586       1.3682461     2.0025756    146.3607750
    rank_mktval   1586       1.8076923     1.4886206     82.3492242
    rank_price    1586       1.7030265     1.3552388     79.5782579
```

The ANOVA Procedure

Class Level Information

Class	Levels	Values
rank_ep	5	0 1 2 3 4

Number of observations   7932

Dependent Variable: hpr5yr   5yr holding period return

Source	DF	Sum of Squares	Mean Square	F Value	Pr > F
Model	4	97.02465	24.25616	8.20	<.0001
Error	7927	23462.04779	2.95976		
Corrected Total	7931	23559.07245			

R-Square	Coeff Var	Root MSE	hpr5yr Mean
0.004118	149.3004	1.720396	1.152305

Source	DF	Anova SS	Mean Square	F Value	Pr > F
rank_ep	4	97.02465410	24.25616352	8.20	<.0001

Each panel corresponds to one level of the RANK_EP variable. For comparison with the next table, we also show the levels of EP and BM across the EP quintiles. Naturally EP increases with its rank, but BM appears to be largely unrelated to it. The more interesting variable, long-term holding period returns, is not monotonically increasing in EP, but it increases substantially in the fifth quintile (largest EP ratio). This increase is also highly significant. (The column "Std Dev" shows the sample standard deviation; hence, to obtain the standard error of the mean, it needs to be divided by the square root of 1586.) The significant difference is confirmed by the ANOVA results: we find that the null of equal returns across quintiles can be rejected at a high level of significance. This is consistent with the hypothesis that a value investment strategy based on the EP ratio outperforms a growth or glamour strategy. Next, we repeat this analysis for portfolios ranked by the book-to-market ratio.

Code 9.5: Univariate analysis of portfolios ranked by the book-to-market ratio

```
* univariate analysis of book-to-market portfolios;
proc sort data=baseranks;
    by rank_bm;
proc means data=baseranks n mean std cv;
    title 'univariate analysis of book-to-market portfolios';
    by rank_bm;
    var ep bm hpr5yr rank_mktval rank_price;
proc anova data=baseranks;
    class rank_bm;
    model hpr5yr = rank_bm;
    quit;
run;
```

Output 9.3: Book-to-market portfolios

```
            univariate analysis of book-to-market portfolios

---------------------------- rank_bm=0 ----------------------------


                         The MEANS Procedure
                                                          Coeff of
     Variable       N          Mean        Std Dev       Variation
     ep          1585       0.0554195      0.0249461      45.0132953
     bm          1585       0.2710328      0.0851932      31.4327948
     hpr5yr      1585       1.0032170      1.4700568     146.5342845
     rank_mktval 1585       2.6340694      1.2323912      46.7865876
     rank_price  1585       2.6063091      1.3186543      50.5946987


---------------------------- rank_bm=1 ----------------------------
                                                          Coeff of
     Variable       N          Mean        Std Dev       Variation
     ep          1586       0.0988295      0.8471680     857.2017275
     bm          1586       0.4686482      0.0685888      14.6354551
     hpr5yr      1586       1.0493965      1.5279827     145.6058437
     rank_mktval 1586       2.2219420      1.3300403      59.8593620
     rank_price  1586       2.1841110      1.3826869      63.3066235


---------------------------- rank_bm=2 ----------------------------
                                                          Coeff of
     Variable       N          Mean        Std Dev       Variation
     ep          1591       1.1989349     44.5725743       3717.68
     bm          1591       0.6456618      0.0800406      12.3966681
     hpr5yr      1591       1.0517317      1.5289891     145.3782420
     rank_mktval 1591       1.9723444      1.3390091      67.8892124
     rank_price  1591       2.0458831      1.3574047      66.3481066


---------------------------- rank_bm=3 ----------------------------
                                                          Coeff of
     Variable       N          Mean        Std Dev       Variation
     ep          1585       0.1079744      0.4593789     425.4515918
     bm          1585       0.8202707      0.1021646      12.4549826
     hpr5yr      1585       1.2010033      1.5125374     125.9394855
     rank_mktval 1585       1.8593060      1.3961584      75.0902989
     rank_price  1585       1.8574132      1.3137231      70.7286367
```

Output 9.3 (continued)

```
------------------------------ rank_bm=4 ------------------------------
                                                       Coeff of
    Variable         N           Mean       Std Dev    Variation
    ep             1585      0.1247524     0.6165878   494.2493308
    bm             1585      9.5477912   126.0624015      1320.33
    hpr5yr         1585      1.4566237     2.3671505   162.5094078
    rank_mktval    1585      1.3148265     1.4235354   108.2679270
    rank_price     1585      1.3110410     1.3669200   104.2621821


                        The ANOVA Procedure

                      Class Level Information

              Class          Levels    Values
              rank_bm             5    0 1 2 3 4

                  Number of observations     7932

Dependent Variable: hpr5yr    5yr holding period return


                            Sum of
Source                  DF      Squares    Mean Square  F Value  Pr > F
Model                    4     218.66461      54.66615    18.57  <.0001
Error                 7927   23340.40784       2.94442
Corrected Total       7931   23559.07245


          R-Square    Coeff Var     Root MSE    hpr5yr Mean
          0.009282     148.9129     1.715931       1.152305

Source                  DF     Anova SS    Mean Square  F Value  Pr > F
rank_bm                  4  218.6646069     54.6661517    18.57  <.0001
```

As displayed above, there is a stronger relation between long-horizon holding period returns and the BM ratio. Returns increase with increasing BM ranks and are significantly different across quintiles; this is again consistent with the hypothesis that a value strategy dominates a growth strategy. On the other hand, this result could at least partially be caused by a size effect, because the larger returns tend to be associated with firms that fall into smaller size (MKTVAL) quintiles. Again, the large holding period returns for high BM portfolios—i.e., value portfolios—indicate a superior return potential for a value investment strategy.

Summary

The purpose of this chapter was to illustrate the simple structure of a SAS program to produce a complex yet persistent result in the literature. In efficient markets, financial accounting information and simple fundamental financial ratios should have no effect on stock returns, because that information is already reflected in the prices of securities. Yet, using only earnings-to-price or book-to-market ratios, we can generate portfolios that yield high returns that persist over long periods. In our sample period, a value investment strategy appeared to outperform a growth or glamour strategy. Although it is not well understood why value strategies outperform growth strategies, the program discussed in this chapter can be easily modified to test new hypotheses that may explain this result.

Program Listing

```
* read crsp and compustat data;
data base;
    infile 'C:\newcrsp.output';
    input cusip $ @10 psdate yymmdd8. @28 hpr5yr @39 price @50 eps @63 bm
@154 mktval;
    format psdate yymmdd6.;
    ep = eps/price;
    yy = year(psdate);
    if bm < 0 then bm = .;
    * keep only records with data for both crsp & compustats;
    if ep = . then delete;
    * labels;

    label hpr5yr = '5yr holding period return';
    label ep = 'earnings-to-price ratio';
    label bm = 'book-to-market ratio';
    label mktval = 'market value of equity';
    label price = 'share price';

proc corr data=base;
    title 'correlation analysis of relevant variables';
    var hpr5yr ep bm mktval price;

* sort by year and create annual quintiles for ep;
proc sort data=base;
    by yy;
proc rank data=base groups=5 out=baseranks;
    var    ep  bm  mktval  price;
    ranks rank_ep rank_bm rank_mktval rank_price;
    by yy;
```

```
* univariate analysis of earnings/price portfolios;
proc sort data=baseranks;
     by rank_ep;
proc means data=baseranks n mean std cv;
     title 'univariate analysis of earnings/price portfolios';
     by rank_ep;
     var ep bm hpr5yr rank_mktval rank_price ;
proc anova data=baseranks;
     class rank_ep;
     model hpr5yr = rank_ep;
     quit;

* univariate analysis of book-to-market portfolios;
proc sort data=baseranks;
     by rank_bm;
proc means data=baseranks n mean std cv;
     title 'univariate analysis of book-to-market portfolios';
     by rank_bm;
     var ep bm hpr5yr rank_mktval rank_price;
proc anova data=baseranks;
     class rank_bm;
     model hpr5yr = rank_bm;
     quit;
run;
```

CHAPTER 10

ANALYSIS OF TRANSACTION DATA

Key Concepts
- Effective spreads
- Information content of trades
- Vector autoregressive models

Data: Annual stock returns and financial statement variables

Background

The microstructure of securities markets has been an exciting topic for financial research over the past 20 years. Transactions data became broadly available in 1988, and with them the number of empirical studies of microstructure increased significantly. Excellent surveys can be found, for example, in O'Hara (1995), who discusses the underlying theories, and Madhavan (2000), who synthesizes empirical research and relates it to the theory.[1]

A wide variety of issues have been on the agenda. Initially, bid-ask spreads were at the forefront, and studies sought to justify their existence and explain their composition. Now it is generally accepted that spreads have three components: order processing cost, inventory cost, and asymmetric information cost. The latter arises because uninformed and informed traders trade in the same market. Since trading is anonymous, market makers protect themselves from informed trading by charging a premium (i.e., a wider spread). Inventory cost arises because when market makers trade, they regularly deviate from their optimal portfolio holdings. Suppose, for example, that a market maker has just made a large purchase of shares. If he was at the optimal inventory level before this trade, he will now be interested in selling part of it. To increase the likelihood that the next trade is a sell from his perspective, he can reduce both the ask price (to make it more likely that some other investor will buy from him) and the bid price (to make it less likely that another investor will sell to him). In this scenario, any sufficiently large trade will move prices and make the next trade in the same direction more expensive. We have evidence that all three components exist, but there is not complete agreement on their relative magnitude.

Another major topic is the optimal design of markets. Several different designs exist in the world, and even within countries different designs compete. For example, in the United States, a specialist/auction market (NYSE) competes with a dealer market (NASDAQ) and purely electronic limit order markets (the ECNs). It is still an open question which features make them work and which markets work best.

Trading costs that institutions and other investors face in securities transactions have also attracted a lot of attention in academic and practitioner journals. It is extremely difficult to obtain precise measures of trading cost. Several reasonable approximations exist, of course, such as effective spreads (discussed below) or similar measures. Available data, however, mostly limit the ability to estimate cost substantially. For example, executed trades are widely available (see below), but orders are not. A significant, if not the most important, component of trading cost, however, is the time it takes for an order to execute. Because researchers typically do not know when orders are submitted, this component is virtually impossible to estimate (some studies using proprietary data come very close).

Related to the topic of trading cost are studies that seek to determine the price impact of a trade. For example, suppose a large trader intends to sell a position of 400,000 shares. He could try to sell all at once. This would generally only be possible at a substantial discount, however, because other market participants may suspect that the trader has (negative) private information about the company. Thus, he will typically split his order into smaller portions of, say, 20,000 shares each to reduce this discount. In this case, his total cost of selling his position would partially depend on how much prices decline in response to these sells. This is because subsequent trades sell at lower prices, if the preceding trades have caused prices to decline.

---

[1] A. Madhavan, "Market Microstructure: A Survey," *Journal of Financial Markets*, 2000; M. O'Hara, *Market Microstructure Theory* (Oxford: Blackwell, 1995).

A good measure of the price impact of a trade would also allow an assessment of how liquid a certain market is. One of the first studies to analyze the relation between trades and prices is Hasbrouck (1991), which uses a vector autoregressive (VAR) model to measure price impacts.[2] In this chapter, our main objective is to illustrate how such estimation is performed in SAS. In addition, we show how to compute different measures of trading cost and how to categorize trades into buys and sells.

The Data

The analysis in this chapter is based on two arbitrarily selected stocks, General Electric and AT&T (stock symbols GE and T). For these stocks, we obtain data from the NYSE's TAQ (Trades and Quotes) database for the first quarter of 1998. We apply the sample code to two securities so it can be easily extended to larger samples. The code makes use of BY-group processing that does not depend on the number of securities in the sample.

The data are originally read from the TAQ data files on WRDS (the appendix to this chapter provides a detailed description of remote processing with SAS/CONNECT). The advantage of using SAS/CONNECT over using telnet to access remote data servers is that the remote and client parts of a program can both run locally. While all processing could have been completed on the remote server, we chose to copy the raw data to the local PC with PROC DOWNLOAD.

All data are initially read into two data sets containing trades and quotes, respectively. For our purposes, the most important *trade* variables are the transaction price, a time stamp, and the trading volume. The most important *quote* information is the bid and ask prices and the time the quote was entered. Additionally, both files contain several variables indicating special cases and errors. We use these indicators to exclude erroneous data and all transactions and quotes outside of official trading hours. Trades are included if they took place on the NYSE or a regional exchange, but we consider only quotes from the "home" exchange, the NYSE (see the appendix for a detailed description). Our variables correspond to the names used in TAQ and are defined as follows:

The trade file (ALLTT1)

SYMBOL	Stock symbol
DATE	Trade date
TIME	Trade time (hh:mm:ss)
PRICE	Actual trade price per share
CORR	Correction indicator
SIZE	Number of shares traded
COND	Sale condition
EX	Exchange on which the quote occurred

---

[2] J. Hasbrouck, "Measuring the Information Content of Stock Trades," *Journal of Finance* 46 (1991): 179-207.

The quote file (ALLQQ1)

```
SYMBOL        Stock symbol
DATE          Quote date
TIME          Quote time (hh:mm:ss)
BID           Bid price
OFR           Offer price
BIDSIZ        Bid size in number of round lots
OFRSIZ        Offer size in number of round lots
MODE          Quote condition
EX            Exchange on which the quote occurred
```

It is important to understand that trades and quote updates take place at different times. Typically, quotes are updated after a trade takes place. However, there are several trades that are not followed by quote changes, and several quote changes that are not preceded by trades. Because the analysis requires both trade and quote data, the first step in the analysis is to reconstruct the timeline of trading activity. We do this by merging trades and quotes in an appropriate manner that reflects the time when each occurred. This is a crucial step for two reasons. First, the right way to merge the data depends on what we intend to do. As you will see, we use a different merging technique for estimating trading costs than for estimating the VAR models. To compute trading costs, we would like to know the quote that was in effect *before* the trade. Thus, the data must be sorted in a way such that each trade is preceded by the prevailing quote when the trade occurred. In contrast, to compute the impact of trades on quote changes, we are primarily interested in how quotes are updated *after* a trade takes place.

Second, the time stamps on trades and quotes are systematically different. The reason is that quotes are entered into the system by the specialist, while trades are entered by exchange clerks. Because his trading profits are at stake, the specialist will usually enter quotes in a very timely manner. In contrast, data on executed trades serve primarily an accounting purpose, and the immediate recording is not as essential as for the quotes. As a result, trades are typically entered with a delay, mostly ranging between 5 and 15 seconds. It apparently has become standard practice to work with a 5-second delay for NYSE firms.

For the VAR analysis, as for several other applications, it is necessary to know whether the buyer or the seller initiated a trade. Because reported trades represent matches of buyers and sellers at a certain price, trade direction cannot be observed directly. The two commonly used procedures to infer trade direction from trade and quote data are the tick test and the quote test (see, for example, Lee and Ready 1991). The tick test classifies a trade as buyer-initiated, if the trade price is above the previous price. Correspondingly, when the current price is below the previous one, the trade is classified as seller-initiated. The quote test compares the current price to the prevailing quote. If the transaction takes place above the quote midpoint, it is deemed buyer-initiated; if it is below the midpoint, it is deemed to be initiated by the seller. In this chapter, we compute both measures and, as suggested by Lee and Ready, use a combination to infer trade direction.

Combining Identical Trades

In a preliminary step, we combine all trades that took place at the same second and price. The underlying intuition is that these individually reported trades are in fact part of the same order, and should therefore be combined (by summing the number of shares). Note that this may not be appropriate for all research questions; for others, the aggregation should be even broader (for example, combining all trades at the same price and minute). Code 10.1 lists the SAS code for the aggregation by price and second.

Code 10.1: Combine trades at the same price and time

```
*** combine all trades at the same time and price into one;
proc sort data=sample.trades out=trades;
    by symbol date time price;
proc means data=trades noprint;
    by symbol date time price;
    output out=adjtrades (rename=(_freq_=numtrades) drop=_type_)
    sum(size)=size;
```

The trades are first sorted by stock, time, and price. Then PROC MEANS is used to sum the trading volume of each individual trade. We use the variable _FREQ_, which is created automatically by PROC MEANS to count the number of trades that were added in this step.

Correcting Time Stamps and Computing the Tick Test

The next preliminary step is to correct the previously discussed reporting delay associated with the trade time. We also compute the necessary variables to perform the tick test.

Code 10.2: Compute tick test and adjust for late trade reporting

```
*** adjust trade time stamp and prepare for tick test;
data ntrades;
    set adjtrades;

    * create unique trade identifier;
    tid = _n_;
    * advance trades by 5 secs to adjust for late reporting;
    time_real = time;
    time = time - 5;
    label time='trade time - 5 secs';
    label time_real = 'reported trade time';
    format time_real time8.;

    * compute variable for tick test;
```

Code 10.2 (continued)

```
* note: this step can be modified to look back further than one trade;
lagprice  = lag(price);
lag2price = lag2(price);
if price > lagprice then tick =  1;
if price < lagprice then tick = -1;
if price = lagprice then do;
        if lagprice > lag2price then tick =  1;
        if lagprice < lag2price then tick = -1;
end;
if _n_ < 3 then tick=0;
if tick = . then tick = 0;
drop time_real lagprice lag2price;
label tick     = 'trade indicator based on tick test';
label tid      = 'trade identifier';
label numtrades = 'number of aggregated trades';
```

This DATA step reads the consolidated trades and creates the new data set NTRADES. The next statement creates a unique trade record identifier, TID. This is very useful for matching purposes.

To adjust the trade time, we subtract five seconds from the reported time and store the difference in the variable TIME. The original time is retained in the variable TIME_REAL for debugging purposes. Next, the tick test variable TICK is computed. Here, we go back two trades to infer trade direction: if the current price is the same as the previous one, we also check the next previous price. You may want to limit this comparison to one price, or extend it to longer intervals, depending on your specific application. If the tick test does not yield an answer, the TICK variable is set to zero. Finally, all new variables are labeled. To check the resulting estimates, PROC FREQ is used to list the frequencies of buys and sells, respectively.

Code 10.3: Frequency analysis for tick test

```
* print frequency counts for tick test;
proc freq data=ntrades;
    by symbol;
    tables tick;
```

The following output reveals that the tick test can classify about two thirds of all trades for both stocks. About one third of trades are classified as buys, and the remaining third as sells.

Output 10.1: Frequency counts for the tick test

```
                        VAR estimation
                quote revisions and order sign

------------------------ Stock Symbol=GE --------------------------

                      The FREQ Procedure
              trade indicator based on tick test

                                    Cumulative     Cumulative
     tick    Frequency     Percent   Frequency      Percent
      -1       47423        32.40      47423         32.40
       0       50312        34.37      97735         66.77
       1       48631        33.23     146366        100.00
                        VAR estimation
                quote revisions and order sign

------------------------ Stock Symbol=T ---------------------------

                      The FREQ Procedure
              trade indicator based on tick test

                                    Cumulative     Cumulative
     tick    Frequency     Percent   Frequency      Percent
      -1       39761        30.35      39761         30.35
       0       52394        40.00      92155         70.35
       1       38837        29.65     130992        100.00
```

Computing Quote Changes and Combining Them with Trades

In this step, we first identify quote changes that also affected the quote midpoint. These midpoint changes are needed for our later analysis of the effect of trades on quote updates. Next, these quotes and all trades are combined into one file. Note that this intermediate step eliminates quote changes from the sample where the midpoint remained the same (for example, when the quoted spread widens symmetrically around the midpoint). In many studies of bid-ask spreads, these spreads may be of particular interest and thus should not be excluded.

Code 10.4: Compute quote changes and combine them with trade records

```
* compute quote changes;
proc sort data=sample.quotes;
    by symbol date time;
data allqchange;
    set sample.quotes;
    by symbol;
    midpoint = (bid+ofr)/2;
    oldmp = lag(midpoint);
    if first.symbol then oldmp = .;
    * create unique quote identifier;
    qid = _n_;

    * output only if the quote has changed;
    drop oldmp;
    label qid     = 'quote identifier';
    label midpoint = 'quote midpoint';
    if midpoint ne oldmp then output;
run;

* combine trades and quotes;
data qandt;
    set allqchange (in=a) ntrades (in=b);
    if a then trade=0;
    if b then trade=1;
```

Code 10.4 reads the quotes and creates a new data set ALLQCHANGE, which contains only quote updates. First, a new variable MIDPOINT is defined as the arithmetic average of the bid and ask quotes. We also create a unique record identifier, QID. Only if the current midpoint is different from the previous one is the record written to the output data set. Again, this procedure is not appropriate for all applications. Here, the primary interest is in the path of quote midpoint; if the spread is of greater importance, you should identify changes of bid *and* ask, and not just those of the midpoint.

The second data step reads the new trade and quote files and combines them into one data set. Note that both share the variables SYMBOL, DATE, and TIME, but both have additional variables that are unique to trades or quotes. We use the SET statement to combine both data sets and create a new indicator variable, TRADE, that classifies each record either as a trade or as a quote. To create this indicator, the data set option IN is used. For example, when set reads a record from NTRADES, the variable B is assigned a value of one. When a quote is read, B is missing. Because the variables created by the IN option are not permanent, their values have to be assigned to a new variable if they need to be written to the output data set; here, both A and B are combined into the TRADE variable.

Note that we use the SET statement and list both the trade and quote data sets in the same statement. This instructs SAS to first read all observations from the first data set, and then all from the second. Thus, the output data set contains all variables that appear in either input data set, and as many observations as both input data sets combined. If a variable appears in only one of the input data sets, its value will be set to missing when records are read from the other input data set. It is important to distinguish the use of a single SET statement with multiple data sets from the use of multiple SET statements, which operate more like (but not identical to) a MERGE statement.

The data set QANDT now contains all quote (midpoint) changes and all aggregated trade records for both GE and AT&T. Most importantly, each record is identified by stock symbol, date, and time, allowing us to subset the data in a way that is useful for our analysis. As discussed earlier in this chapter, the procedure to do that depends on the type of questions we need to answer. We first present a solution to the trading-cost estimation, and later one for the VAR analysis.

Estimation of Trading Costs

To estimate measures of trading cost, we are interested in the quotes that were posted at the time a trade was executed (ideally, the quote at the time the order was entered, but those data are not public). Thus, the data set QANDT only needs to be sorted by date and time for each security. Because the data contain all quote changes, after sorting, the most recent quote record that precedes a certain trade is the prevailing quote for this trade. The only complication is that often one or more trades follow each other without intervening quote changes; this has to be accounted for.

Code 10.5: Compute net order flow and various spread measures

```
*** sort and compute spreads;
title1 'Spread estimation';

proc sort data=qandt;
    by symbol date time;

data spread;
    set qandt;
    by symbol date;

    * reset retained variables if a new ticker or new day starts;
    if first.symbol or first.date then do;
    nbid = .; nofr = .; currentmidpoint = .; end;

    * assign bid and ask to new variables for retaining;
    if bid     ne . then nbid            = bid;
    if ofr     ne . then nofr            = ofr;
    if midpoint ne . then currentmidpoint = midpoint;
```

Code 10.5 (continued)

```
* compute spread measures;
effsprd = abs(price - (nbid+nofr)/2) * 2;
asprd   = nofr - nbid;
rsprd   = asprd / price;

*** compute variables for trade direction;
if currentmidpoint ne . then do;

* quote test - compare current trade to quote: -1 is a sell, +1 is a buy;
     if price < currentmidpoint then ordersign = -1;
     if price > currentmidpoint then ordersign =  1;
     * tick test for midpoint trades;
     if price = currentmidpoint then do;
          if tick =  1 then ordersign =  1;
          if tick = -1 then ordersign = -1;
          if tick =  0 then ordersign =  0;
     end;
     * signed net order flow;
     nof = ordersign * size;
end;

* labels;
label nbid      = 'last outstanding bid';
label nofr      = 'last outstanding ofr';
label effsprd   = 'effective spread';
label asprd     = 'absolute spread';
label rsprd     = 'relative spread';
label nof       = 'net order flow';
label ordersign = 'indicator for trade direction';

* output to data set;
if trade=1 then output spread;
retain nbid nofr currentmidpoint;
drop bid ofr midpoint qid trade;
```

The program first sorts the data by stock, date, and time. The sorted records are then read in BY groups corresponding to the sorting. This technique has the advantage that SAS automatically marks the first and last record for each of those groups; these indicators will be used by the program. The basic programming intuition is to first check whether a record is a quote or a trade. If it is a quote, it will be retained. If the next record is again a quote, the new record will overwrite the old retained one. On the other hand, if the next record is a trade, the retained variables (the prevailing quote) will be added to the trade record and then written to the output data set SPREAD.

The first step is to initialize the retainer variables NBID, NOFR, and CURRENTMIDPOINT. Whenever the first record of a stock or of a new day is read, they are set to missing. Next, they are assigned the current values of bid, ask, and midpoint, respectively. Note that the "IF BID (OFR, MIDPOINT) NE." conditions are satisfied only by quote records; trade records all have missing values there. Thus, these statements always assign the most recent quotes to the retainer variables.

Next, the program computes three spread measures, the effective, absolute, and relative spreads. The absolute spread is defined as the dollar difference between ask and bid, and the relative spread is additionally scaled by the midpoint. The effective spread is based on the difference between trade price and midpoint. It is computed as twice the absolute value of this difference.

To infer trade direction, the third section of the code applies a combined quote and tick test to trade records. The new variable ORDERSIGN is set to one (minus one) if the trade price is above (below) the prevailing quote midpoint. For trades at the midpoint, the previously computed tick test is applied. Finally, the signed net order flow is computed as the product of ORDERSIGN and SIZE, the trading volume of each transaction.

After assigning the appropriate labels to each new variable, all trade records (which now include the prevailing quotes) are written to the new data set SPREAD. Note the RETAIN statement below the OUTPUT statement; it tells SAS not to set all variables to missing before it reads the next record from the input data set. Instead, the current values of the retainer variables are preserved.

The following PROC MEANS statement is used to produce descriptive statistics for each stock.

Code 10.6: Compute descriptive statistics for net order flow and spread measures

```
proc means data=spread n mean median min max;
    by symbol;
    var price size effsprd asprd rsprd ordersign nof;
```

The output is shown in the table below (labels are omitted to save space). It is always important to check outliers in the data. For example, the table for GE shows that the absolute spread becomes as large as $1.00; this is very large compared to the mean of about 8.7 cents. When checking this observation in the original data, you will find that this and more large estimates mostly appear around the opening of trading on February 3, 1998. Depending on your application, you may want to go into greater detail in verifying that these numbers indeed represent spreads that were quoted at those times and not potential data errors. Similarly, the huge effective spread of $1.94 may be due to a mismatch of quotes and trades or due to a data entry error. It is important for most applications that these extreme values be checked.

Output 10.2: Descriptive statistics for spreads and net order flow

```
                              VAR estimation
                        quote revisions and order sign

    ----------------------------- SYMBOL=GE ------------------------------------

                              The MEANS Procedure

    Variable        N           Mean         Median        Minimum        Maximum
    PRICE       146366     77.4458148     77.2500000     70.2500000     87.6250000
    size        146366        1624.95    500.0000000    100.0000000    2041500.00
    effsprd     145997      0.0690562      0.0625000              0      1.9375000
    asprd       145997      0.0866105      0.0625000      0.0625000      1.0000000
    rsprd       145997      0.0011214     0.000823045    0.000713267      0.0129870
    ordersign   145997     -0.0267882              0     -1.0000000      1.0000000
    nof         145997    172.5460112              0     -486100.00      619400.00


    ----------------------------- SYMBOL=T -------------------------------------

    Variable        N           Mean         Median        Minimum        Maximum
    PRICE       130992     63.1927131     63.1875000     57.3750000     68.5000000
    size        130992        2386.97    500.0000000    100.0000000    1137800.00
    effsprd     130730      0.0623709      0.0625000              0      2.0625000
    asprd       130730      0.1007984      0.1250000      0.0625000      0.4375000
    rsprd       130730      0.0015990      0.0018744    0.000913242      0.0070281
    ordersign   130730     -0.1704047     -1.0000000     -1.0000000      1.0000000
    nof         130730    382.0393177    -100.0000000    -1000000.00     1137800.00
```

VAR Estimation

In this subsection, we first discuss the elaborate programming elements that line up the data for the VAR estimation. Next, we estimate the VAR model.

Arranging the Data for Use in the VAR Estimation

Recall that we are interested in quote changes that take place after trades, as opposed to the quote prevailing at the time of the trade. More specifically, we would like to match each trade with the quote change that took place within 15 seconds of the trade. If there was no change, we will assign a zero quote change to the trade record. This procedure will also leave several quote changes that are not assigned to trades; this will happen whenever there was no trading within the 15 seconds prior to the quote update. We also would like to add these updates to the output data and to assign zero trading volume to these records.

Following this basic logical flow, the first step is to find quote changes after trades. Unfortunately, the SAS DATA step naturally reads data sequentially—it is cumbersome and inefficient to use direct access to read forward. To avoid the need to look forward, we simply re-sort the QANDT data set backward in time. This intermediate step allows us to look forward in time by accessing previously read records.

Code 10.7: Re-sort trades and quotes in reverse time

```
*** Code to merge for VAR estimation;
*** Program logic:
  - if quote record, then retain the relevant variables
  - if quote record, and previous was also a quote, then assign an
orderflow of zero
  - if trade record, and time between last quote and trade is <= 15 secs,
then there was a new quote within 15 secs AFTER the trade (it is sorted
backward in time) -  assign retained quote to this trade record
  - if trade record and the previous was also a trade, then the associated
quote change should be zero - this is achieved by simply retaining the
most recently read quote (use lag, not retained);

* sort backward in time to match trades to subsequent quote changes;
proc sort data=qandt;
    title1 'VAR estimation';
    by symbol descending date descending time descending qid;
```

This PROC SORT statement sorts stocks in ascending sequence, but within each stock it sorts time stamps in descending sequence. Note that we use the unique quote identifier QID to break potential ties. This may be necessary because below we use QID in a merge statement. Next, we use a DATA step to create the new trade/quote records for the VAR analysis.

Code 10.8: Determine quote updates associated with prior trades

```
* associate order flow with quote changes in trade time;
data tradematch;
    set qandt;
    by symbol descending date;
    lagtrade = lag(trade);
    lagsymbol= lag(symbol);

    * reset retained variables if a new ticker or new day starts;
    if first.symbol and first.date then do;
    /* if desired, reset values to missing for nbid, nofr, etc here for
each day */
    end;

    *** quote records;
    * assign bid and ask to variables for retaining if quote data is
nonmissing (it is here always missing by construction);
    if trade = 0 then do;
          nbid=bid; nofr=ofr; nqid=qid; qtime=time; nmidpoint=midpoint;
    end;

    *** trade records;
    * ask and bid then are the most recent outstanding quote;
    if trade = 1 and lagtrade=0 and symbol=lagsymbol then do;
    /* omitting lagtrade=0 fills preceding trades with wrong subsequent
quote info */
          qage = qtime - time;
          if qage <= 15 then do; /* change here for different lead time*/
              bid  = nbid;
              ofr  = nofr;
              qid  = nqid;
              midpoint = nmidpoint;
          end;
          * labels and formats;
          format qtime time8.;
    end;
    label bid   = 'last outstanding bid';
    label ofr   = 'last outstanding ofr';
    label qtime = 'time of last quote';
    label qage  = 'delay between trade and quote';
    retain nbid nofr qtime nmidpoint nqid;
    drop nmidpoint nbid nofr nqid lagsymbol lagtrade trade;
    * output;
    if trade = 1 then output tradematch;
```

The DATA step creates the new data set TRADEMATCH and reads all observations from QANDT, which is now sorted differently than it was in the previous section. The DATA step is again processed in BY groups to facilitate access to the first and last records in each group. The program begins by defining new variables for the lagged trade indicator and the lagged stock symbol. While not necessary as the program is written now, it is generally a good idea to proceed that way. The reason is that if the LAG function is called in conditional statements, it will not operate as expected. For most purposes, it only works properly when it is executed for each new observation that is read from the input data set. The next (commented) statement allows the user to reset values, such as those of the lagged variables, for different days.

The next statements ("quote records") read only quote records and retain the values of bid, offer, quote identifier, quote time, and midpoint. This is similar to the previous section, but here the subsequent quote, not the previous quote, is retained. Subsequently ("trade records") we begin lining up quote changes with trades. The first case to handle is when trades are directly followed by quotes (note that when two trade records are adjacent, the former has caused no quote change).

The variable QAGE measures the time difference between trade and quote. Because we are only interested in quote updates within 15 seconds of the trade, we assign the retained quote data only then to the trade record. Notice that if no quote update follows the trade within this period, the quote variables still have missing values. This has to be taken into account later when the midpoint changes are computed for each trade record: these missing values indicate zero quote change and need to be converted accordingly. After the label statements, the RETAIN statement tells SAS not to reset the retainer variables and to drop certain variables that are not necessary in the output data set. Note that some variables appear in both the RETAIN and DROP statements. This is done intentionally, and it accomplishes two tasks. First, it makes the current value of those variables available to the next iteration of the data step (instead of assigning a missing value to each variable before reading the new record). Second, at the same time, the DROP statement prevents this variable from being written to the output data set (to conserve disk space and to speed computations). Thus, the RETAIN-DROP combination for the same variable retains its value in memory, but does not require disk space in the output file. Finally, all trade records (now including any quote updates within 15 seconds) are written to the output data set.

This DATA step has now selected all quote updates that have followed trades. It is possible, however, that some quote changes occurred that were not preceded by trades; those would not be included in TRADEMATCH. Thus, it is necessary to add nonmatched quotes to the data. To do that, we first identify all nonmatched quotes.

Code 10.9: Find quote updates not associated with trades

```
* identify all unique quotes matched to a trade within x seconds;
proc sort data=tradematch (keep=qid qage where=(qage ne . and qage<=15))
out=qids nodupkey;
    /* change here also for different lead time */
    by qid;

* merge with all original quotes and retain only those not already matched
with trades;
data quotematch;
    merge allqchange (in=a) qids (in=b drop=qage);
    by qid;
    if not b;
```

In the preceding statements, PROC SORT is used with the options OUT= and NODUPKEY. The former instructs the procedure to write the sorted file to a new data set QIDS (by default, the original data set is replaced). The latter eliminates all duplicate occurrences of the sort key—in this case, it results in a list of all unique quotes that are contained in the TRADEMATCH data. The WHERE option selects only those observations where QAGE has a nonmissing value not exceeding 15 seconds (this is redundant, because quote data should be missing when these conditions are not satisfied, but retained as a precaution).

Next, the list of "used" quotes is merged with the data set ALLQCHANGE, which contains all quote updates. Only quotes that are not contained in the QIDS list are written to the new output data set QUOTEMATCH. Thus, we now have a list of all quote changes that have not occurred within 15 seconds of a trade and are therefore not matched to a trade record. We would like to include them as separate records associated with zero trading volume in the VAR analysis below.

Code 10.10: Add unmatched quote updates to the trade-and-quote data set

```
* combine unmatched quotes with those already matched to trades;
* this adds one record for each unmatched quote;

data qnspread;
    set tradematch (drop=bid ofr price numtrades size qtime)
    quotematch (in=new);
    unmatchedquote = new;

proc sort data=qnspread;
    by symbol date time qid;

* compute midpoint changes;
data allqncspread;
    set qnspread;
    by symbol;
    if not first.symbol then do;
/* add code to prevent mpret computation overnight if desired*/
            if midpoint ne . then currentmidpoint = midpoint;
            mpret = currentmidpoint - lag(currentmidpoint);
    end;
    retain currentmidpoint;
    drop currentmidpoint;
```

The first DATA step uses the SET statement to combine the matched trade records with unmatched quote updates. The new variable UNMATCHEDQUOTE indicates all unmatched quotes for debugging and error-checking purposes. The output data set QNSPREAD is then sorted by stock, date, and time.

The main purpose of the second DATA step is to compute the quote changes for each record. Note that the IF condition that the MIDPOINT not be missing is not redundant. The data set TRADEMATCH (see Code 10.8) contains missing values for MIDPOINTs whenever a trade was not followed by a quote update within 15 seconds. By default, SAS propagates missing values. This means that the result of any computation that involves a missing value will also be missing. In this case, a series of missing values for MIDPOINT would result in a series of missing values for MPRET. Instead, for the subsequent estimation MPRET should be zero in those cases. Thus, in this step the computation is using only nonmissing MIDPOINTs.

The final step in the preliminary data organization is to add the trade-direction variables to the data. Trade direction was estimated above and is in the data set SPREAD. These variables are now merged into the ALLQNCSPREAD data set using the unique trade identifier TID as a merge key.

Code 10.11: Add trade-direction variables to the trade-and-quote data and compute descriptive statistics

```
*** add trade-direction variables to this data set;
proc sort data=allqncspread;
    by tid;

data sample.vardata;
    merge allqncspread (keep=symbol date time tid unmatchedquote mpret)
        spread (keep=tid nof ordersign tick);
    by tid;
    * set trade-direction variables to zero for all quote changes without
trades;
    if unmatchedquote then do;
            nof  = 0;
            tick = 0;
            ordersign = 0;

    end;
    label mpret     = 'change in quote midpoint';
    label nof       = 'net order flow';
    label ordersign = 'nof sign - combined quote and tick test';
    label tick      = 'nof sign - tick test';
    drop unmatchedquote;

proc sort data=sample.vardata;
    by symbol date time;

* summary statistics;
proc means data=sample.vardata n mean median min max;
    var mpret tick nof ordersign;
    by symbol;
```

Recall that we have added quote changes to the data that were not associated with any trades. Those records have missing values for all trade variables, although we would like to treat them as records with zero trading volume. The three assignment statements in Code 10.11 do exactly that. Finally, the data are sorted by stock and time and are now ready for the time-series analysis. The next output shows some descriptive statistics for the final data set VARDATA (labels are omitted).

Output 10.3: Descriptive statistics for quote-update model

```
                              VAR estimation

- - - - - - - - - - - - - - - - - - - - SYMBOL=GE - - - - - - - - - - - - - - - - - - - - - - - - - -

                           The MEANS Procedure

Variable        N          Mean      Median      Minimum      Maximum
mpret      152243   0.000084158           0   -1.8125000    0.9375000
tick       152254     0.0079341           0   -1.0000000    1.0000000
nof        151885   165.8570629           0   -486100.00     619400.00
ordersign  151885    -0.0257497           0   -1.0000000    1.0000000


- - - - - - - - - - - - - - - - - - - - - SYMBOL=T - - - - - - - - - - - - - - - - - - - - - - - - -

Variable        N          Mean      Median      Minimum      Maximum
mpret      134038  -0.000152709           0  -27.5937500    1.3437500
tick       134039    -0.0068935           0   -1.0000000    1.0000000
nof        133777   373.3377187  -100.0000000  -1000000.00   1137800.00
ordersign  133777    -0.1665234   -1.0000000   -1.0000000    1.0000000
```

Potentially important for further analysis, the reported means do not reflect the true means. This is because, by construction, several zero-change records have been added to the data set. Moreover, the quote changes show relatively large extreme values. This is because the code allows computations from one day's close to the next day's open—further inspection reveals that all large quote changes occur over the weekend or overnight. Depending on the application, it may be necessary to exclude such data points.

Estimating the VAR Model

Finally, the data are ready to perform the VAR analysis. Closely following Hasbrouck (1991), we estimate the following model:

$$
x_t = \alpha_0 + \sum_{i=1}^{p} \alpha_{t-i}^{x} x_{t-i} + \sum_{t=1}^{p} \alpha_{t-i}^{r} r_{t-i} + u^x
$$

$$
r_t = \gamma_0 + \gamma_t^x x_t + \sum_{i=1}^{p} \gamma_{t-i}^{x} x_{t-i} + \sum_{t=1}^{p} \gamma_{t-i}^{r} r_{t-i} + u^r
$$

(10.1)

In this model, x represents net order flow, and r represents changes in the quote midpoint. The error terms u^x have mean zero and variance $\sigma_x^2 I$, and correspondingly for u^r.[3] It should be pointed out that this is not an ad hoc model; rather, it is carefully founded on theoretical considerations (see Hasbrouck 1991). This has the advantage that we get some

---

[3] Hasbrouck (1991) estimates the model without an intercept term, using a trade-direction indicator in place of net order flow. Because net order flow may not have a mean of zero, we initially include the intercept terms.

guidance for estimating the system. For example, the above assumption about the variance of u allows us to estimate model (10.1) using OLS. The theory does not, however, provide guidelines for the optimal lag length p. Furthermore, it is not clear that our sample data result in stationary and mean-zero series, which would eliminate the need to include trend variables and constant terms in the regression equations. Thus, before estimating the actual model, we perform a simple specification check for lag length, test for the presence of a linear trend, and assess the need for an intercept term. In practice, depending on the application, these checks should be more elaborate and address the specific issues associated with the data.

Code 10.12: Specification check for the VAR model

```
* preliminary analysis and specification tests;
proc varmax data=sample.vardata (where=(mpret ne . and nof ne .));
    by symbol;
    title2 'specification check';
    model nof, mpret / p=0 trend=linear method=ls printform=univariate;
    output lead=0;
```

These statements estimate model (10.1) using OLS. The WHERE option requests that only records with nonmissing values be read; missing values are not permissible in this procedure. The procedure automatically generates each equation of the model that needs to be estimated. In this specific case, it will generate two equations (one with quote changes, MPRET, and one with net order flow, NOF, as the dependent variable). The independent variables are controlled by the options P=0 and TREND=LINEAR. The former requests that the procedure determines the optimal lag length for the model by minimizing the Akaike Information Criterion (one could also use a larger value for P, maybe 20, and then use the TEST option to the MODEL statement to test whether certain lags have zero coefficients). The TREND option requests a linear trend term. If model (10.1) is specified correctly, both this trend variable and the intercepts should have zero coefficients. Option METHOD=LS further instructs the procedure to use an OLS estimator for all coefficients. Finally, option PRINTFORM instructs the procedure to print the estimated coefficients variable by variable, and not in matrix form.

The resulting output (not shown) yields three important observations:

1. The optimal lag length is five; thus, we will estimate the model with five lags.
2. The coefficient of the trend variable is not significantly different from zero in either equation; thus, we do not include a trend variable in the model.
3. The intercept coefficient in the quote equation is zero, as we would expect if quote changes are, on average, zero. In contrast, it is significantly positive in the order-flow equation; therefore, we will include an intercept for both equations in our estimation.

It turns out, however, that neither of these choices has notable effects on the impulse responses that we estimate below. This could certainly be sample specific—it is important to investigate the effects of different assumptions on the results very carefully.

Computing the Impulse Response Functions

An impulse response function shows how one variable reacts to changes ("innovations") in another variable in the system. Because model (10.1) is a dynamic system, a change in X (net order flow) would affect future values of both X and R (quote changes)—and vice versa. Using the estimated coefficients of (10.1), it is possible to compute the permanent effects of such responses. Based on the previous discussion, we employ a two-equation VAR model using five lags and no trend. We estimate the model with OLS and include an intercept term.

Code 10.13: Vector autoregressive regression model

```
* estimation of orthogonalized impulse responses;
proc varmax data=sample.vardata (where=(mpret ne . and nof ne .));
    by symbol;
    title2 'quote revisions and net order flow';
    model nof, mpret / p=5 method=ls printform=univariate
print=(impulse=(orth));
    output lead=0;
```

Most options are as in the diagnostic run in the previous section, except that P=5 requests an estimation with five lags. In this case, we are interested not in the coefficients, but rather in the orthogonalized impulse responses that describe how the system reacts to shocks to the underlying (structural) system. This is the purpose of the PRINT= option, which requests orthogonalized impulse responses. PROC VARMAX then computes the responses to a one-standard-deviation structural shock to each variable. Note that the ordering in the MODEL statement is not important for the coefficient estimates. Most interest, however, usually lies in the orthogonalized impulse responses; there the ordering does matter. Specifically, putting NOF before MPRET allows current values of the quote change to depend on current values of net order flow, but not vice versa. Note that this reflects the way the data was set up: each record represents a trade and the associated subsequent quote change.

The following table presents the impulse responses of the corresponding output. Note that PROC VARMAX produces substantially more output (including the estimates of model coefficients, AR-coefficients, covariance matrices, cross-correlations, and several diagnostics) that we have not reproduced here.

Output 10.4: Orthogonalized impulse responses for net order flow and quote updates

```
                              VAR estimation
                       quote revisions and net order flow

-------------------------- Stock Symbol=GE --------------------------

                           The VARMAX Procedure

                    Number of Observations          151885
                    Number of Pairwise Missing           0

Variable  Type  NoMissN       Mean      StdDev         Min         Max
nof       DEP    151885   165.85706        4897     -486100      619400
mpret     DEP    151885   0.0000998     0.01948    -1.06250     0.90625


Variable  Label
nof       net order flow
mpret     change in quote midpoint


            Orthogonalized Impulse Response by Variable

            Variable    Lead          nof          mpret
            nof            0    4802.91981              0
                           1     942.11825      -48.45581
                           2     176.26027      -13.17661
                           3      92.32818        1.91691
                           4      83.22661       27.90290
                           5      96.74020       37.37853
                           6      37.25573        4.41375
                           7      13.31721        0.45755
                           8       7.46365        0.50512
                           9       5.80960        0.84624
                          10       4.15178        0.82732
                          11       1.78144        0.24585
                          12       0.76609        0.08799
            mpret          0       0.00137        0.01930
                           1       0.00168     -0.00099190
                           2    0.00080162     -0.00018092
                           3    0.00044281     -0.00013650
                           4    0.00052573     -0.00009492
                           5    0.00058001      0.00006227
                           6    0.00012304      0.00000855
                           7    0.00003981      0.00000673
                           8    0.00002348      0.00000547
                           9    0.00001985      0.00000592
                          10    0.00001622      0.00000424
```

Output 10.4 (continued)

```
                          11    0.00000655    5.787341E-7
                          12    0.00000288    2.030481E-7



-------------------------- Stock Symbol=T -----------------------------

                  Number of Observations        133777
                  Number of Pairwise Missing          0

Variable  Type   NoMissN        Mean      StdDev         Min         Max
 nof      DEP     133777    373.33772        8309    -1000000     1137800
 mpret    DEP     133777   -0.0001362     0.07725   -27.59375     1.34375


Variable  Label
 nof      net order flow
 mpret    change in quote midpoint

               Orthogonalized Impulse Response by Variable

          Variable    Lead          nof          mpret
          nof            0    8268.94373              0
                         1     610.53278      302.96660
                         2     248.64079      159.11999
                         3     291.25641       47.42941
                         4     150.85565       50.39155
                         5     101.84106       21.65062
                         6      36.21542       11.16710
                         7      19.53246        6.06430
                         8      11.50101        3.22528
                         9       6.06600        1.73135
                        10       3.15374        0.87650
                        11       1.58054        0.46323
                        12       0.84455        0.24550
          mpret          0       0.00110        0.01649
                         1       0.00108     0.00031859
                         2    0.00059569     0.00011192
                         3    0.00065026     0.00028392
                         4    0.00039509     0.00023456
                         5    0.00028686     0.00005014
                         6    0.00008680     0.00002815
                         7    0.00005176     0.00001857
                         8    0.00003305     0.00000956
                         9    0.00001720     0.00000469
                        10    0.00000853     0.00000240
                        11    0.00000430     0.00000130
                        12    0.00000236     6.855297E-7
```

The results appear reasonably well behaved in that the impulse responses decay over the 12 lags shown in the output. The responses of quote changes (MPRET) to net order flow are positive, and therefore they are consistent with the idea that net order flow has information content. Specifically, positive net order flow (buy orders exceed sell orders) causes quotes to increase immediately, and also in subsequent periods. For example, in the AT&T example, a one-standard-deviation increase in NOF increases quotes immediately by $0.0011. Additionally, the same increase in order flow also has longer-term consequences, because the quotes show further increase reactions throughout the 12 lags shown here. Thus, there is information content in trades and the specialist reacts to this information.

Program Listing

```
*** Program to read TAQ data, compute spreads, and estimate a VAR model;

*** combine all trades at the same time and price into one;
proc sort data=sample.trades out=trades;
    by symbol date time price;
proc means data=trades noprint;
    by symbol date time price;
    output out=adjtrades (rename=(_freq_=numtrades) drop=_type_)
sum(size)=size;

*** adjust trade time stamp and prepare for tick test;
data ntrades;
    set adjtrades;

    * create unique trade identifier;
    tid = _n_;
    * advance trades by 5 secs to adjust for late reporting;
    time_real = time;
    time = time - 5;
    label time='trade time - 5 secs';
    label time_real = 'reported trade time';
    format time_real time8.;

    * compute variable for tick test;
    * note: this step can be modified to look back further than one trade;
    lagprice  = lag(price);
    lag2price = lag2(price);
    if price > lagprice then tick =  1;
    if price < lagprice then tick = -1;
    if price = lagprice then do;
        if lagprice > lag2price then tick -  1;
        if lagprice < lag2price then tick = -1;
    end;
```

```
if _n_ < 3 then tick=0;
    if tick = . then tick = 0;
drop time_real lagprice lag2price;
    label tick     = 'trade indicator based on tick test';
    label tid      = 'trade identifier';
    label numtrades = 'number of aggregated trades';
* print frequency counts for tick test;
proc freq data=ntrades;
    by symbol;
    tables tick;


* compute quote changes;
proc sort data=sample.quotes;
    by symbol date time;
data allqchange;
    set sample.quotes;
    by symbol;
    midpoint = (bid+ofr)/2;
    oldmp = lag(midpoint);
    if first.symbol then oldmp = .;
    * create unique quote identifier;
    qid = _n_;

    * output only if the quote has changed;
    drop oldmp;
    label qid      = 'quote identifier';
    label midpoint = 'quote midpoint';
    if midpoint ne oldmp then output; run;


* combine trades and quotes;
data qandt;
    set allqchange (in=a) ntrades (in=b);
    if a then trade=0;
    if b then trade=1;


*** sort and compute spreads;
title1 'Spread estimation';

proc sort data=qandt;
    by symbol date time;

data spread;
    set qandt;
    by symbol date;
```

```
* reset retained variables if a new ticker or new day starts;
if first.symbol or first.date then do;
nbid = .; nofr = .; currentmidpoint = .; end;

* assign bid and ask to new variables for retaining;
if bid      ne . then nbid            = bid;
if ofr      ne . then nofr            = ofr;
if midpoint ne . then currentmidpoint = midpoint;

* compute spread measures;
effsprd = abs(price - (nbid+nofr)/2) * 2;
asprd   = nofr - nbid;
rsprd   = asprd / price;

*** compute variables for trade direction;
if currentmidpoint ne . then do;

* quote test - compare current trade to quote: -1 is a sell, +1 is a
buy;
        if price < currentmidpoint then ordersign = -1;
        if price > currentmidpoint then ordersign =  1;
        * tick test for midpoint trades;
        if price = currentmidpoint then do;
            if tick =  1 then ordersign =  1;
            if tick = -1 then ordersign = -1;
            if tick =  0 then ordersign =  0;
        end;
        * signed net order flow;
        nof = ordersign * size;
end;

* labels;
label nbid      = 'last outstanding bid';
label nofr      = 'last outstanding ofr';
label effsprd   = 'effective spread';
label asprd     = 'absolute spread';
label rsprd     = 'relative spread';
label nof       = 'net order flow';
label ordersign = 'indicator for trade direction';

* output to data set;
if trade=1 then output spread;
retain nbid nofr currentmidpoint;
drop bid ofr midpoint qid trade; run;

proc means data=spread n mean median min max;
    by symbol;
    var price size effsprd asprd rsprd ordersign nof; run;
```

```
*** Code to merge for VAR estimation;
*** Program logic:
  - if quote record, then retain the relevant variables
  - if quote record, and previous was also a quote, then assign an
orderflow of zero
  - if trade record, and time between last quote and trade is <= 15 secs,
then there was a new quote
    within 15 secs AFTER the trade (it is sorted backward in time) -
assign retained quote to this trade record
  - if trade record and the previous was also a trade, then the associated
quote change should be zero - this is achieved by simply retaining the
most recently read quote (use lag, not retained);

* sort backward in time to match trades to subsequent quote changes;
proc sort data=qandt;
    title1 'VAR estimation';
    by symbol descending date descending time descending qid;

* associate order flow with quote changes in trade time;
data tradematch;
    set qandt;
    by symbol descending date;
    lagtrade = lag(trade);
    lagsymbol= lag(symbol);

    * reset retained variables if a new ticker or new day starts;
    if first.symbol and first.date then do;
    /* if desired, reset values to missing for nbid, nofr, etc here for
each day */
    end;

    *** quote records;
    * assign bid and ask to variables for retaining if quote data is
nonmissing (it is here always missing by construction);
    if trade = 0 then do;
        nbid=bid; nofr=ofr; nqid=qid; qtime=time; nmidpoint=midpoint;
    end;

    *** trade records;
    * ask and bid then are the most recent outstanding quote;
    if trade = 1 and lagtrade=0 and symbol=lagsymbol then do;
    /* omitting lagtrade=0 fills preceding trades with wrong subsequent
quote info */
        qage = qtime - time;
        if qage <= 15 then do; /* change here for different lead time*/
            bid  = nbid;
            ofr  = nofr;
```

```
                        qid  = nqid;
                        midpoint = nmidpoint;
                end;
                * labels and formats;
                format qtime time8.;
        end;
        label bid   = 'last outstanding bid';
        label ofr   = 'last outstanding ofr';
        label qtime = 'time of last quote';
        label qage  = 'delay between trade and quote';
        retain nbid nofr qtime nmidpoint nqid;
        drop nmidpoint nbid nofr nqid lagsymbol lagtrade trade;
        * output;
        if trade = 1 then output tradematch;

* identify all unique quotes matched to a trade within x seconds;
proc sort data=tradematch (keep=qid qage where=(qage ne . and qage<=15))
out=qids nodupkey;
        /* change here also for different lead time */
        by qid;

* merge with all original quotes and retain only those not already matched
with trades;
data quotematch;
        merge allqchange (in=a) qids (in=b drop=qage);
        by qid;
        if not b;

* combine unmatched quotes with those already matched to trades;
* this adds one record for each unmatched quote;

data qnspread;
        set tradematch (drop=bid ofr price numtrades size qtime)
        quotematch (in=new);
        unmatchedquote = new;

proc sort data=qnspread;
        by symbol date time qid;

* compute midpoint changes;
data allqncspread;
        set qnspread;
        by symbol;
        if not first.symbol then do;
/* add code to prevent mpret computation overnight if desired*/
                if midpoint ne . then currentmidpoint = midpoint;
                mpret = currentmidpoint - lag(currentmidpoint);
        end;
        retain currentmidpoint;
```

```
        drop currentmidpoint;

*** add trade-direction variables to this data set;
proc sort data=allqncspread;
     by tid;

data sample.vardata;
     merge allqncspread (keep=symbol date time tid unmatchedquote mpret)
           spread (keep=tid nof ordersign tick);
     by tid;
     * set trade-direction variables to zero for all quote changes without
trades;
     if unmatchedquote then do;
           nof  = 0;
           tick = 0;
           ordersign = 0;
     end;
     label mpret     = 'change in quote midpoint';
     label nof       = 'net order flow';
     label ordersign = 'nof sign - combined quote and tick test';
     label tick      = 'nof sign - tick test';
     drop unmatchedquote;

proc sort data=sample.vardata;
     by symbol date time;

* summary statistics;
proc means data=sample.vardata n mean median min max;
     Var mpret tick nof ordersign;
     by symbol;

*** VAR model;

* preliminary analysis and specification tests;
proc varmax data=sample.vardata (where=(mpret ne . and nof ne .));
     by symbol;
     title2 'specification check';
     model nof, mpret / p=0 trend=linear method=ls printform=univariate;
     output lead=0;

* estimation of orthogonalized impulse responses;
proc varmax data=sample.vardata (where=(mpret ne . and nof ne .));
     by symbol;
     title2 'quote revisions and net order flow';
     model nof, mpret / p=5 method=ls printform=univariate
print=(impulse=(orth));
     output lead=0;

run;
```

Appendix: Using SAS/CONNECT Software to Access WRDS

This appendix describes in detail how to use SAS/CONNECT software to access WRDS. As an example, we discuss the program statements that are used to extract the TAQ data used in Chapter 10. The setup described here assumes that SAS is installed locally on a PC (configuring a local mainframe or UNIX installation would require similar steps, but the paths would be different). To use SAS/CONNECT, the remote server also needs to run SAS; it is not necessary that both sites run the same version of SAS.

Preliminary SAS Setup

The first two steps configure SAS for remote access to WRDS. It is necessary to copy a login script and to modify the SAS configuration files.

Updating the SAS Configuration File

The configuration file is always located in the sasroot directory. In Version 8, this is typically C:\Program Files\SAS Institute\SAS\V8 (in prior versions, it was C:\Sas). It is a basic text file that is named SASV8.CFG (or CONFIG.SAS in earlier versions). SAS executes the statements in the configuration file when it is started. To use remote access to WRDS, the following two lines should be added at the beginning of the configuration file:

```
-remote wrds
-comamid tcp
```

Be sure to include the leading hyphens.

Updating the AUTOEXEC.SAS File

In some installations, it is necessary to add three lines to the AUTOEXEC.SAS file. This file resides in the sasroot directory and is executed automatically when SAS starts up. If the file does not already exist, it can be created using any plain-text editor with the following content:

```
filename rlink '!sasroot\connect\saslink\tcpwrds.scr';
%let wrds=wrds.wharton.upenn.edu;
run;
```

Installing the Communication Script

The necessary communication script can be downloaded from http://wrdsx.wharton.upenn.edu/support/downloads. The current filename is tcpwrds_scr.zip. This archive contains a brief documentation and the script file *tcpwrds.scr*. All that remains to be done is to copy this file into the directory that houses the SAS/CONNECT scripts— typically, this is C:\Program Files\SAS Institute\SAS\V8\connect\saslink in Version 8. You are now ready to use remote processing.

Obtaining TAQ Data from WRDS

Before remote processing can be used, you need to connect your machine to the remote server. To do that, choose the SIGNON command from the RUN menu and hit ENTER on the next form (leave it blank unless you regularly use different remote connections). On the second form, just enter your WRDS username and password. Now your local SAS program can communicate with the remote SAS program, and you can read data sets or execute other programs remotely.

To obtain the TAQ data necessary for Chapter 10, we have used the following program statements. Please note that part of the following code (the macro) is a modified version of a sample program downloaded from WRDS. The first statement is RSUBMIT; it instructs SAS to execute the following statements remotely. Once SAS encounters the ENDRSUBMIT statement, it continues processing locally. If necessary, you can go back and forth as often as needed. The second statement is an X instruction, which executes a command on the remote host. In this case it is a UNIX server, and we would like to create a temporary directory to store some output data sets. The new directory is named SAMPLE99 and is located in the current temporary storage area on WRDS (this might change over time). Next, the library SAMPLE is assigned to this new directory, and the TAQ files are assigned to the library TAQ.

Code 10.14: Remote access to WRDS to obtain data from TAQ

```
*** Use SAS/Connect to access TAQ on WRDS and create a file for
downloading;

*** Start remote execution and assign remote WRDS libraries;
*** NOTE: create remote folder 'sample' first (using telnet, ftp, or the
SAS X command);
rsubmit;
x 'mkdir /sastemp/sample99';
libname sample '/sastemp/sample99';

/* This macro is based on the macro taq.sas, written by Steve Crispi and
Benjamin Marcus, 7/97,
   Wharton Computing & Information Technology Core Systems & Data Services

   INPUTS
   - file: specify CT (Consolidated Trade) or CQ (Consolidated Quote)
   - bdate:specify beginning date in SAS date format ('ddmmmyy'd)
   - edate:specify ending date in SAS date format ('ddmmmyy'd)
   - query:specify ticker symbols, each enclosed in double-quotes and
                separated by a space, e.g.: "A" "AA" "AAA"
   - out:  Specify a name for output SAS data set to be stored

   VARIABLES
       Name        TYPE    FILE        Variable Label
       SYMBOL      char    CT & CQ     Stock Symbol
       DATE        num     CT & CQ     Quote date
       TIME        num     CT & CQ     Quote time
       BID         num          CQ     Bid Price
       PRICE       num     CT          Actual Trade Price per Share
       OFR         num          CQ     Offer Price
       SIZE        num     CT          Number of Shares Traded
       BIDSIZ      num          CQ     Bid size in number of round lots
       G127        num     CT          Comb G Rule 127 and Stop Stock
indicator
```

Code 10.14 (continued)

```
      CORR      num          CT      Correction Indicator
      OFRSIZ    num          CQ      Offer size in number of round lots
      COND      char     CT          Sale condition
      MODE      num          CQ      Quote condition
      EX        char     CT & CQ     Exchange on which the quote occurred
      MMID      char         CQ      Identifies the NASDAQ market maker
*/

%macro taqq(file,bdate,edate,query,out);
%local num i;
* Get names of files range;
data _null_;
    call symput('bfile',"&file"||put(&bdate,yymmdd4.));
    call symput('efile',"&file"||put(&edate,yymmdd4.));

* Get a list of all TAQ SAS data sets;
proc datasets library=taq memtype=data;
    contents out=work.temp(keep=memname) data=_all_ noprint;

* Designate the data sets that are needed (assign to macro vars);
data _null_;
    set temp end=final;
    by memname notsorted;
    where memname between "&bfile" and "&efile";
    if last.memname;
    n+1;
    if final then call symput('num', put(n,8.));
    call symput('v'||left(put(n,8.)),trim(memname));

* Create an empty data set for accumulating results;
data temp;
    set _null_;
* Gather the data needed from each data set;
%do i=1 %to &num;
    data &&v&i;
        set taq.&&v&i;
        where symbol in (&query) and date between &bdate and &edate;
    data temp;
        set temp &&v&i;
%end;

* Save the SAS data set;
data sample.&out;
    set temp; run;
%mend taqq;
```

Code 10.14 (continued)

```
* invoke macro twice to obtain trades and quotes;
%taqq(CT,'01jan98'd,'31mar98'd,"GE" "T",allt);
%taqq(CQ,'01jan98'd,'31mar98'd,"GE" "T",allq);
*** subset TAQ trade data;
data sample.trades;
    set sample.allt (where=(ex in ('A','B','C','M','N','P','X')
                            and cond in ('','*')
                            and corr in (0,1)
                            and time < hms(16,05,00)
                            and time > hms(9,30,00)));
    keep symbol date time price size;

data sample.quotes;
    set sample.allq (where=(ex in ('A','N')
                            and (ofrsiz>0 or bidsiz>0)
                            and ofr>bid
                            and mode in(3,10,12)
                            and time < hms(16,05,00)
                            and time > hms(9,30,00)));
    keep symbol date time bid ofr;

* download data to local library - requires that library SAMPLE exist on
remote and local system;
proc download data=sample.trades;
proc download data=sample.quotes; run;

endrsubmit;
```

Next, the macro TAQQ is defined. The macro is self-explanatory; the required inputs are the type of data sought. The WRDS Web site has some additional documentation on its usage. In the example above, TAQQ is used to read one quarter of trades and quotes for AT&T and General Electric, respectively. The macro is also instructed to write the result to the data sets SAMPLE.ALLT and SAMPLE.ALLQ.

In the subsequent DATA step, these files are read and selected data are written to the new data sets SAMPLE.TRADES and SAMPLE.QUOTES. From the trade file, we first select trades on six exchanges and NASDAQ. Next, we select only trades that have condition codes equal to blank or "*" and correction codes equal to 0 or 1. Further, we require that the trade took place during official trading hours (we allow an additional five minutes after the official close). Only trades that meet these criteria are written to the output data set ALLT1.

Quotes are included only if they originate on either AMEX or the NYSE to avoid auto quotes from the regionals and third-market quotes from NASDAQ market makers. We drop observations that have zero depth on both sides, and we eliminate crossed/locked quotes (where the ask is not larger than the bid). Additionally, only quotes during official trading hours are selected, and they must have MODE equal to 3, 10, or 12 (see the TAQ manual for details on the variables).

Finally, the resulting data sets can be downloaded to the local machine. In the example, we use PROC DOWNLOAD to do that. This procedure is part of SAS/CONNECT and is used to transfer data between the remote and local SAS sessions.

REFERENCES

Altman, Edward. 1968. "Financial Ratios, Discriminant Analysis, and the Prediction of Corporate Bankruptcy." *Journal of Finance* 23: 589-609.

Ball, R., and P. Brown. 1968. "An Empirical Evaluation of Accounting Income Numbers." *Journal of Accounting Research* 6: 159-178.

Basu, S. 1977. "Investment Performance of Common Stocks in Relation to Their Price Earnings Ratios: A Test of the Efficient Market Hypothesis." *Journal of Finance* 32: 663-682.

Black, F. 1972. "Capital Market Equilibrium with Restricted Borrowing." *Journal of Business* (July): 444-455.

Boehmer, Ekkehart, Annette Poulsen, and Jim Musumeci. 1991. "Event Study Methodology under Conditions of Event-Induced Variance." *Journal of Financial Economics* 30: 253-272.

Broussard, John Paul, David Michayluk, and Walter Neely. 2000. "The Role of Growth in Long Term Investment Returns." Working paper.

Chen, N.-F., R. Roll, and S. A. Ross. 1986. "Economic Forces and the Stock Market." *Journal of Business* 59 (3): 383-402.

Collins, W., and S. P. Kothari. 1989. "An Analysis of Intertemporal and Cross-Sectional Determinants of Earnings Response Coefficients." *Journal of Accounting and Economics* 11 (2/3): 143-181.

Conrad, J., and G. Kaul. 1993. "Long-Term Market Overreaction or Biases in Computed Returns." *Journal of Finance* 48 (1): 39-64.

DeBondt, W., and R. Thaler. 1985. "Does the Stock Market Overreact?" *Journal of Finance* 40: 793-805.

Fama, E., and K. French. 1992. "The Cross Section of Expected Stock Returns." *Journal of Finance* 46: 427-466.

Fama, E. F., and J. MacBeth. 1973. "The Cross-Section of Expected Stock Returns." *Journal of Finance* 47 (2): 427-465.

Fama, E. F., L. Fischer, M. Jensen, and R. Roll. 1969. "The Adjustment of Stock Prices to New Information." *International Economic Review* 10: 1-21.

Hasbrouck, J. 1991. "Measuring the Information Content of Stock Trades." *Journal of Finance* 46: 179-207.

Haugen, R. A. 1995. *The New Finance: The Case against Efficient Markets.* Englewood Cliffs, NJ: Prentice Hall.

Henderson, Glenn V., Jr. 1990. "Problems and Solutions in Conducting Event Studies." *Journal of Risk and Insurance* 57: 282-306. Reviews of basic event-study methodology.

Judge, G. G., W. E. Griffiths, R. C. Hill, H. Luetkepohl, and T. C. Lee. 1985. *The Theory and Practice of Econometrics*. 2d ed. New York: Wiley.

Kahya, Emel, and Panayiotis Theodossiou. 1999. "Predicting Corporate Financial Distress: A Time-Series CUSUM Methodology." *Review of Quantitative Finance and Accounting* 13: 323-345.

Kothari, S. P. 1992. "Price-Earnings Regressions in the Presence of Prices Leading Earnings: Earnings Levels versus Change Specifications and Alternative Deflators." *Journal of Accounting and Economics* 15: 173-202.

Kothari, S. P., and J. L. Zimmerman. 1995. "Price and Return Models." *Journal of Accounting and Economics* 20: 155-192.

Lakonishok, J., A. Shleifer, and R. W. Vishny. 1994. "Contrarian Investment, Extrapolation, and Risk." *Journal of Finance* 49: 1541-1578.

Lee, Charles, and Mark Ready. 1991. "Inferring Trade Direction from Intradaily Data." *Journal of Finance* 46: 733-746.

Lintner, John. 1965. "Security Prices, Risk, and Maximal Gains from Diversification." *Journal of Finance* 20: 587-615.

Lo, Andrew, and Craig MacKinlay. 1988. "Stock Market Prices Do Not Follow Random Walks: Evidence from a Simple Specification Test." *Review of Financial Studies* 1: 41-66.

Madhavan, A. 2000. "Market Microstructure: A Survey." *Journal of Financial Markets* 3: 205-258.

O'Hara, M. 1995. *Market Microstructure Theory*. Oxford: Blackwell.

Patell, J. 1976. "Corporate Forecasts of Earnings per Share and Stock Price Behavior: Empirical Tests." *Journal of Accounting Research*, 14 (2): 246-276.

Peterson, Pamela P. 1989. "Event Studies: A Review of Issues and Methodology." *Quarterly Journal of Business and Economics* 28 (3): 36-66.

Shanken, J. 1992. "The Current State of the Arbitrage Pricing Theory." *Journal of Finance* 47 (4): 1569-1575.

Sharpe, William F. 1964. "Capital Asset Prices: A Theory of Market Equilibrium under Conditions of Risk." *Journal of Finance* 19: 425-442.

Theodossiou, Panayiotis, Emel Kahya, Reza Saidi, and George Philippatos. 1996. "Financial Distress and Corporate Acquisitions: Further Empirical Evidence." *Journal of Business Finance and Accounting* 23: 699-719.

White, H. 1980. "A Heteroskedasticity-Consistent Covariance Matrix Estimator and a Direct Test for Heteroskedasticity." *Econometrica* 48: 817-838.

Index

Books Available from SAS Press

Advanced Log-Linear Models Using SAS®
by **Daniel Zelterman**

Analysis of Clinical Trials Using SAS®: A Practical Guide
by **Alex Dmitrienko, Geert Molenberghs, Walter Offen,** *and*
Christy Chuang-Stein

Annotate: Simply the Basics
by **Art Carpenter**

*Applied Multivariate Statistics with SAS® Software,
Second Edition*
by **Ravindra Khattree**
and **Dayanand N. Naik**

*Applied Statistics and the SAS® Programming Language,
Fifth Edition*
by **Ronald P. Cody**
and **Jeffrey K. Smith**

An Array of Challenges — Test Your SAS® Skills
by **Robert Virgile**

*Carpenter's Complete Guide to the SAS® Macro Language,
Second Edition*
by **Art Carpenter**

The Cartoon Guide to Statistics
by **Larry Gonick**
and **Woollcott Smith**

*Categorical Data Analysis Using the SAS® System,
Second Edition*
by **Maura E. Stokes, Charles S. Davis,**
and **Gary G. Koch**

Cody's Data Cleaning Techniques Using SAS® Software
by **Ron Cody**

*Common Statistical Methods for Clinical Research with
SAS® Examples, Second Edition*
by **Glenn A. Walker**

The Complete Guide to SAS® Indexes
by **Michael A. Raithel**

*Data Management and Reporting Made Easy with
SAS® Learning Edition 2.0*
by **Sunil K. Gupta**

*Debugging SAS® Programs: A Handbook of Tools and
Techniques*
by **Michele M. Burlew**

*Efficiency: Improving the Performance of Your SAS®
Applications*
by **Robert Virgile**

The Essential Guide to SAS® Dates and Times
by **Derek P. Morgan**

The Essential PROC SQL Handbook for SAS® Users
by **Katherine Prairie**

*Fixed Effects Regression Methods for Longitudinal Data
Using SAS®*
by **Paul D. Allison**

Genetic Analysis of Complex Traits Using SAS®
Edited by **Arnold M. Saxton**

A Handbook of Statistical Analyses Using SAS®, Second Edition
by **B.S. Everitt**
and **G. Der**

Health Care Data and SAS®
by **Marge Scerbo, Craig Dickstein,**
and **Alan Wilson**

The How-To Book for SAS/GRAPH® Software
by **Thomas Miron**

*In the Know ... SAS® Tips and Techniques From
Around the Globe*
by **Phil Mason**

Instant ODS: Style Templates for the Output Delivery System
by **Bernadette Johnson**

*Integrating Results through Meta-Analytic Review Using
SAS® Software*
by **Morgan C. Wang**
and **Brad J. Bushman**

Learning SAS® in the Computer Lab, Second Edition
by **Rebecca J. Elliott**

The Little SAS® Book: A Primer
by **Lora D. Delwiche**
and **Susan J. Slaughter**

The Little SAS® Book: A Primer, Second Edition
by **Lora D. Delwiche**
and **Susan J. Slaughter**
(updated to include Version 7 features)

The Little SAS® Book: A Primer, Third Edition
by **Lora D. Delwiche**
and **Susan J. Slaughter**
(updated to include SAS 9.1 features)

The Little SAS® Book for Enterprise Guide 3.0
by **Susan J. Slaughter**
and **Lora D. Delwiche**

Logistic Regression Using the SAS® System: Theory and Application
by **Paul D. Allison**

Longitudinal Data and SAS®: A Programmer's Guide
by **Ron Cody**

Maps Made Easy Using SAS®
by **Mike Zdeb**

Models for Discrete Data
by **Daniel Zelterman**

Multiple Comparisons and Multiple Tests Using SAS®
Text and Workbook Set
(books in this set also sold separately)
by **Peter H. Westfall, Randall D. Tobias, Dror Rom, Russell D. Wolfinger,** and **Yosef Hochberg**

Multiple-Plot Displays: Simplified with Macros
by **Perry Watts**

Multivariate Data Reduction and Discrimination with SAS® Software
by **Ravindra Khattree** and **Dayanand N. Naik**

Output Delivery System: The Basics
by **Lauren E. Haworth**

Painless Windows: A Handbook for SAS® Users, Third Edition
by **Jodie Gilmore**
(updated to include Version 8 and SAS 9.1 features)

The Power of PROC FORMAT
by **Jonas V. Bilenas**

PROC SQL: Beyond the Basics Using SAS®
by **Kirk Paul Lafler**

PROC TABULATE by Example
by **Lauren E. Haworth**

Professional SAS® Programmer's Pocket Reference, Fifth Edition
by **Rick Aster**

Professional SAS® Programming Shortcuts, Second Edition
by **Rick Aster**

Quick Results with SAS/GRAPH® Software
by **Arthur L. Carpenter** and **Charles E. Shipp**

Quick Results with the Output Delivery System
by **Sunil K. Gupta**

Reading External Data Files Using SAS®: Examples Handbook
by **Michele M. Burlew**

Regression and ANOVA: An Integrated Approach Using SAS® Software
by **Keith E. Muller** and **Bethel A. Fetterman**

SAS® for Forecasting Time Series, Second Edition
by **John C. Brocklebank** and **David A. Dickey**

SAS® for Linear Models, Fourth Edition
by **Ramon C. Littell, Walter W. Stroup,** and **Rudolf J. Freund**

SAS® for Mixed Models, Second Edition
by **Ramon C. Littell, George A. Milliken, Walter W. Stroup,** and **Russell D. Wolfinger**

SAS® for Monte Carlo Studies: A Guide for Quantitative Researchers
by **Xitao Fan, Ákos Felsővályi, Stephen A. Sivo,** and **Sean C. Keenan**

SAS® Functions by Example
by **Ron Cody**

SAS® Guide to Report Writing, Second Edition
by **Michele M. Burlew**

SAS® Macro Programming Made Easy
by **Michele M. Burlew**

SAS® Programming by Example
by **Ron Cody** and **Ray Pass**

SAS® Programming for Researchers and Social Scientists, Second Edition
by **Paul E. Spector**

SAS® Programming in the Pharmaceutical Industry
by **Jack Shostak**

SAS® Survival Analysis Techniques for Medical Research, Second Edition
by **Alan B. Cantor**

SAS® System for Elementary Statistical Analysis, Second Edition
by **Sandra D. Schlotzhauer** and **Ramon C. Littell**

SAS® System for Regression, Third Edition
by **Rudolf J. Freund** and **Ramon C. Littell**

SAS® System for Statistical Graphics, First Edition
by **Michael Friendly**

The SAS® Workbook and *Solutions* Set
(books in this set also sold separately)
by **Ron Cody**

Selecting Statistical Techniques for Social Science Data: A Guide for SAS® Users
by **Frank M. Andrews, Laura Klem, Patrick M. O'Malley, Willard L. Rodgers, Kathleen B. Welch,** and **Terrence N. Davidson**

Statistical Quality Control Using the SAS® System
by **Dennis W. King**

*A Step-by-Step Approach to Using the SAS® System
for Factor Analysis and Structural Equation Modeling*
by **Larry Hatcher**

*A Step-by-Step Approach to Using SAS® for Univariate and
Multivariate Statistics, Second Edition*
by **Norm O'Rourke, Larry Hatcher,**
and **Edward J. Stepanski**

Step-by-Step Basic Statistics Using SAS®: Student Guide
and *Exercises*
(books in this set also sold separately)
by **Larry Hatcher**

*Survival Analysis Using SAS®:
A Practical Guide*
by **Paul D. Allison**

*Tuning SAS® Applications in the OS/390 and z/OS
Environments, Second Edition*
by **Michael A. Raithel**

*Univariate and Multivariate General Linear Models:
Theory and Applications Using SAS® Software*
by **Neil H. Timm**
and **Tammy A. Mieczkowski**

Using SAS® in Financial Research
by **Ekkehart Boehmer, John Paul Broussard,**
and **Juha-Pekka Kallunki**

Using the SAS® Windowing Environment: A Quick Tutorial
by **Larry Hatcher**

Visualizing Categorical Data
by **Michael Friendly**

Web Development with SAS® by Example
by **Frederick Pratter**

Your Guide to Survey Research Using the SAS® System
by **Archer Gravely**

JMP® Books

*JMP® for Basic Univariate and Multivariate Statistics: A Step-by-
Step Guide*
by **Ann Lehman, Norm O'Rourke, Larry Hatcher,**
and **Edward J. Stepanski**

JMP® Start Statistics, Third Edition
by **John Sall, Ann Lehman,**
and **Lee Creighton**

Regression Using JMP®
by **Rudolf J. Freund, Ramon C. Littell,**
and **Lee Creighton**